ABOUT THE AUTHOR

After taking her Masters in Asian St[...]
Edie Irwin travelled to India where she me[...]
studied psychotherapy with him in London for five years. Her
interests later broadened to therapeutic massage and Tibetan
painting and, in 1979, she moved to the Borders of Scotland to
train with Dr Akong Tulku Rinpoche at Samye Ling, the oldest
Tibetan Buddhist centre in the West. During the 1980s she helped
develop a therapy programme at the centre and to train therapists
and then, in 1993, embarked on a three-year retreat. Recently, she
has divided her time mostly between the States and the UK, and
between therapeutical and humanitarian work.

Healing Relaxation

♥

*Seven key steps to
dissolving tension and
enjoying life*

E D I E   I R W I N

RIDER

LONDON • SYDNEY • AUCKLAND • JOHANNESBURG

1 3 5 7 9 10 8 6 4 2

Copyright © Tara Rokpa Edinburgh (ROKPA TRUST, U.K.) 1999

First published in 1999 by Rider,
an imprint of Ebury Press, Random House,
20 Vauxhall Bridge Road, London SW1V 2SA
www.randomhouse.co.uk

Random House Australia (Pty) Limited
20 Alfred Street, Milsons Point, Sydney,
New South Wales 2061, Australia

Random House New Zealand Limited
18 Poland Road, Glenfield,
Auckland 10, New Zealand

Random House South Africa (Pty) Limited
Endulini, 5A Jubilee Road,
Parktown 2193, South Africa

Random House UK Limited Reg. No. 954009

Illustrations by Marita Wiemer

Papers used by Rider are natural, recyclable products made from wood
grown in sustainable forests.

Printed and bound by Mackays of Chatham plc, Kent

A CIP catalogue record for this book
is available from the British Library

ISBN 0-7126-7032 -7

Contents

To all our parents and
all parents
everywhere in all times.

Foreword

Looking over the collection of drafts and notes from which I find myself working to complete this book, I follow a paper trail going back to 1980, with an intensive collection dating from November 1993 to August 1995. The early notes are records of relaxation courses that I presented at the request of Dr Akong Tulku Rinpoche, first in Edinburgh and at Kagyu Samye Ling in Scotland. The later are from presentations to groups in eight European countries, USA and Canada, Australia, Southern Africa and India. This frenetic activity came to an abrupt end in 1993, when I entered a traditional three year and three month Tibetan Buddhist enclosed meditation retreat at Kagyu Samye Ling.

In the run-up to my retreat I worked furiously to complete the manuscript of this book. I had begun the book at the request of many participants of courses who had asked for something they might take home in order to be able to carry on with the work. It was meant especially for the use of my colleagues: Dorothy Gunne, Carol Sagar, Brion Sweeney and Trish Swift, who were more and more taking up the travelling portion of the work of Tara Rokpa Therapy in addition to their presentation of Akong Rinpoche's therapy work in their own localities. As I headed for the retreat they were also on the verge of launching the first Tara Rokpa Therapy Training for which I was assured these notes would be useful to trainees as they began the work of initiating and supporting groups of people wishing to do the Tara Rokpa Therapy.

Less than a fortnight away from the proposed three years of voluntary incarceration and with the book still largely in note form, I met my friend Colin Betts. An accomplished writer and fellow-collaborator in the editing of the previous book of Akong Tulku Rinpoche, *Taming the Tiger*, Colin asked if I had any works in progress that could use a helping hand. I was enormously grateful not just for the kind thought but the veritable offer of rescue. I passed on all I had written so far: three finished chapters, stacks of notes and 16 hours of audio tapes which I was still dictating an hour before entry into retreat! Colin was actually the first person, as well as the most persuasive, in insisting that the book was worthy of general publication. We left it that he would take the book as far as he could, including publication if possible.

Colin had carried the book four chapters further down the road when well-wishers, eager to see the book published quickly, persuaded him to surrender the manuscript. On the advice of Akong Tulku Rinpoche, it was then set aside until the finish of my retreat.

Up to this point it was not only Colin, but Paul Gilbert of Samye Ling, who had contributed large amounts of donated time to transcribing tapes and Carol Johnson of Carlisle who had volunteered the typing of handwritten pages during the last days of her life.

In early 1997, I began to work on the manuscript once again, as my colleagues in the Tara Rokpa Therapy impressed upon me the need for the text as a workbook for trainees setting up groups undertaking Beginning to Relax, which is the first stage of the Tara Rokpa Therapy and a prerequisite for joining a 'Back to Beginnings' Tara Rokpa Therapy group. More information about Tara Rokpa Therapy is available at the end of this book. I was very grateful to Maggy Jones of Samye Ling for typing some additions and corrections during the months before I was able to purchase a laptop computer to get on with the work. At this stage, friends in Dublin, Pat Murphy and David Casby, contributed photographs and sample drawings as a notable first effort at illustration.

I was very soon drawn away from the contemplative space of retreat and increasingly engaged in the actual work of the Tara Rokpa Therapy which had evolved so rapidly in my absence. I met frequently with my colleagues, who struggled to bring me up to speed with changes and developments. I joined the faculty of Tara Rokpa Therapy Training. Again and again it was impressed upon me that the text for Beginning to Relax was needed for our work. I was also moved once again by the many positive responses to our work, especially from people of all backgrounds for whom this was a first contact with visualisation, relaxation and massage. I began reluctantly sharing round draft copies for the use of Tara Rokpa therapists only. I was thus extremely grateful to Judith Kendra at Rider Books when she phoned requesting a look at the manuscript. Her response was encouraging and we agreed that the book could be pulled together quite quickly with a bit more work.

Though the rewriting has not been great, it has been most interesting applying myself to this material after the three year retreat. Going some distance into one of the world's most profound paths of spiritual development has brought me round to greater respect for whatever is simple. I love this work for its accessibility and feel inordinately blessed to have spent most of my adult life sharing it with others. May it prove to be of great benefit to all who undertake any part of it.

Introduction

Has anyone ever ordered you to, 'RELAX!'? It doesn't work, does it? We know that tension gets in the way of our truly enjoying life, but we don't know how to let go. We may even try to justify our tension saying, 'If I were to relax completely, I'd fall apart.'

My motive in writing this guide is threefold. It is a response to requests from massage and therapy clients; to support those interested in doing 'Back to Beginnings' (a therapeutic process developed by Akong Tulku Rinpoche together with me and other Tara Rokpa therapists), and also to give a simple outline of relaxation exercises and massage techniques for use by anyone who may be interested.

I began teaching exercises in relaxation and massage in 1978, in Washington DC. For the last 18 years I have tried to develop my work following the teachings and guidance of Akong Tulku Rinpoche. Akong Tulku Rinpoche is a Tibetan Buddhist Lama and physician trained in Tibetan medicine who has been living in Scotland for more than thirty years, applying his knowledge and skills to the relief of suffering of all those who seek his help. He is the founder of Rokpa Trust, an international charity whose slogan is 'Helping where help is needed', and of Tara Rokpa, which consists of subsidiaries of the main trust dedicated to the development of all forms of medicine and therapy based on compassion. The Edinburgh Tara Trust (the progenitor of Tara Rokpa, Edinburgh), and a series of relaxation courses in Edinburgh dating back to the early eighties, have provided a main testing ground for this work and I would like to thank all who have been involved in its development.

Akong Tulku Rinpoche first gave me advice about the practice of massage in 1977. We had just met and I told him that I practised massage for a living. He told me it was his hobby, but that he only knew one kind of massage that worked. Eager to receive transmission of some secret Oriental technique, I asked, 'What kind of massage would that be?' 'Compassion,' he replied.

At first I felt tricked and disappointed. Compassion? It's just a word. I thought I was going to learn an effective technique. Over the next few years I came to realise that the advice he had given me was truthful and practical. Nothing I did for a person at a physical level would really touch them unless I genuinely cared for their well-being. If I didn't take the trouble to leave aside my own concerns and open up to how they were feeling, then the time would largely be wasted and little of true value would flow.

It was also challenging advice because I realised I didn't really know the meaning of the word 'compassion'; least of all 'universal compassion' or 'non-expectation compassion'. These seemed to be as far beyond me as Enlightenment. And yet, I did want my practice of massage to be effective. So I had to continue to relate to Rinpoche's assertion that compassion is the only massage that works. I had to ask myself again and again: what is my motivation?

The Tibetan medical tradition arises from a truly holistic vision of reality. For all intents and purposes, from the time of conception to the time of death, the mind and body are considered to be as one. Further, each person is like a cell in the body of the planet Earth, which is a cell in the body of the Universe. Everything we need to be whole and healthy is available if we know how to find it and how to use it. Much illness and suffering is based on states of imbalance, which are set in motion by the presence of mental poisons. These poisons are ignorance, which keeps us from knowing what we need; passion, which causes us to want and try to take more than we need; and aggression, which causes us to reject or destroy what is needed.

In Tibetan language, the word sowa means simultaneously: to repair damage or redress an imbalance and to protect from damage and prevent imbalance occurring in the first place. For example, we may notice a thinning of the wool at the elbow of a favourite jumper and find a matching yarn to reinforce it before a hole appears. Or we may do nothing about it until there's a little hole and then mend it with the appropriate yarn. However, if we wait until there is a gaping hole, we will have to use some kind of patch. All three are sowa, appropriate to different stages and conditions of damage.

The exercises and advice in this rough guide are really very simple and probably nothing new to many people. They are meant to repair the strain and tension brought about by the conditions of modern life, and to give suggestions of ways to prevent them happening in the first place, by learning to relax.

Much of what is presented here was taught to me by Akong Tulku Rinpoche to be passed on to others. Some I learned along the way from friends and teachers who practise massage of many types, as well as yoga, tai chi and aikido. I have also learned over the years from many books. However, whatever is here I have made my own through practice, and thus feel confident to pass it along as something that might be of benefit to others.

Why do we generally feel relaxed when we're happy and happy when we relax? No doubt there is an explanation for this based on brain and body chemistry. However this is beyond my knowledge so I can only look at it from the commonsense point of view. When I'm happy nothing worries me, so I can relax. Somehow it relates to my mind – especially my outlook or motivation. When I wish myself well and wish nobody else any harm then I tend to be happy. In this state I am also more able to accept things as they are: myself, others and the world. If my intention is to be happy and to help others to be happy and to try not to harm anyone, then although I may be very active and face many difficulties, on the whole I won't be worried because I'll know I'm doing the best I can.

It's simple! So why can't I just live like this, happy and relaxed? The short answer is that I have these persistent bad habits, tense stressful habits such as rushing around, worrying, wanting, avoiding, indulging, deploring, blaming and so on. Often the pace and complexity of modern life makes me forget that I'm not obliged to carry on like this – pushed around by habits that make me tense, so that I'm little use to myself or others.

As human beings we have the right and ability to change our attitude, our approach, our habits. We are allowed to relax and be happy, but first we might need to create opportunities actually to experience these fortunate states of being for ourselves – we might have to work at it a little.

COULD THIS BOOK HELP YOU?

Are you a person who is aware that tension may be getting in the way of being able to appreciate life fully? Then you may well be someone who can benefit from this book. Even if you do not feel able to follow a practice plan in a structured way, you may still be able to try out some of the exercises or even just test the ideas against your own experience. Thinking clearly about our lives is at least as important as learning to massage or stretch or visualise. Especially if you work in a health or caring field, you may find something in this book which helps you to do your work in a way which is more effective and more satisfying.

In past times and places it may be that the knowledge of finding relaxation within an ordinary working day was commonplace. There are still individuals who have a special gift for finding ease wherever they are and usually they also help to create an environment which is relaxing for others. I think we can all bring to mind places we enjoy visiting because there is such a good atmosphere. It may be the home of a friend, a doctor's surgery, a corner café, a bank or office of some kind. I remember once working in a small cheesecake factory where the work was grueling, but the atmosphere was great. What made it so? The manager had a gift for letting people be themselves and do the work in their own rhythm. This was based on his ability to be aware of the needs of cheesecakes in the oven and people baking them at the same time. He also encouraged all of us to learn every facet of the work so we could easily allow each other breaks as needed. We played word games, we sang, and we got to know each other. The key factor that allowed this to happen was a relaxed atmosphere arising from a relaxed attitude. My hope is that this book may help you to see how you can bring a little more of this natural relaxation into your life.

The session plans and suggestions which follow may give you some idea of how to adapt the material in this book for your personal use. They are also designed for those wishing to help each other as well as themselves by forming a group and working with this book. This may be a group of friends or colleagues or those with similar personal problems. In fact, any group of people interested in creating relaxation and happiness in the world may find the exercises beneficial.

OUTLINE OF SESSIONS

The main chapters of this book are organised in the form of sessions, which may form a lesson or meeting plan for as many people as wish to participate. There will be six sessions, each of which could be covered in one period of about two to three hours. However, if you are getting together as a self-help group, I would recommend that you be prepared to go more slowly or be satisfied to leave out some of each session. There is nothing quite so unrelaxing as trying to keep to a fixed schedule. My experience of presenting this material is that as people get more into it, it goes more slowly. So don't feel you and your friends are doing something wrong if you find the suggested lessons are too long. Just try to be creative in adapting to the needs and schedules of all the members of the group in finding a solution.

At the end it is suggested that if you have been meeting as a group, you should plan a full day to put together all the massage elements, as well as the key methods of relaxation. If you are working with this book on your own, the relaxation methods, warm-up exercises and self-massage will be particularly useful. Those exercises which can be done on your own are marked with a ♥ throughout this book.

If you are in poor health, have any recent or long-standing injuries, are pregnant or very advanced in years, it is important that you should take care with each new exercise. If you have doubts as to whether or not an exercise will be beneficial for you or not, it's probably best to leave it out. ★ indicates those exercises that are quite strenuous and should be approached with caution or left out entirely. The general contra-indications for massage are given in the Introduction on pages 28–30 and should be studied carefully.

SESSION ONE: PAGES 33–53

Basic breathing exercise ♥

WARMING-UP ♥

SHOULDERS AND ARMS
Shrug and relax
Folded-arms circles
Finger-linked ceiling stretch

WRISTS
The jumping fish ★
Falling leaf stretch ★
Hand flapping

HANDS
Exploring hands
Raising and sensing warmth in the hands

SELF-MASSAGE OF THE SHOULDERS, ARMS AND HANDS ♥

SHOULDERS AND ARMS
Shoulder to chest stroke
Kneading the shoulder muscles
Warming the shoulders
Warming the arms

HANDS
Exploring fingers
The palm
The back of the hand
Linked hands: thumb to palm pressure

GROUP WORK
Friendliness exercise

EXCHANGING A HAND MASSAGE

SESSION TWO: PAGES 54–65

Breathing exercise ♥
Feeling exercise ♥

ROOTEDNESS AND SLOW WALKING ♥ ★
Rootedness exercise
Slow walking

WARMING-UP

SELF-MASSAGE OF THE FEET ♥
Foot massage

SESSION THREE: PAGES 66–77

BENEFITS OF THE WHITE LIGHT EXERCISE

THE WHITE LIGHT VISUALISATION ♥
Practising the visualisation

LIMP
The game of Limp ★

EXCHANGING A FOOT MASSAGE
Giving a foot massage

SESSION FOUR: PAGES 78–100

BREATHING AND FEELING ♥

GROUP WORK
Back-to-back ★

SELF-HELP FOR THE BACK ♥
Swinging from the waist and hanging off the wall ★
Knee-to-chest
The pelvic tilt
The rocking chair ★

SESSION FIVE: PAGES 101–31

Moving down the spine
Across the back
Finishing off

SESSION SIX: PAGES 132–49

THE BLUE LIGHT VISUALISATION ♥
Introducing the blue light
Extending the visualisation
A personal experience

GROUP WORK
Pushing hands

SELF-MASSAGE OF THE LEGS AND ABDOMEN ♥
Leg warmer
The upper legs
Standing knee rotation
The abdomen ★

EXCHANGING A NECK AND HEAD MASSAGE ★
Beginning the head massage
The neck and shoulders
Working deeper into the shoulder blades
Returning to the shoulders and arms
Finishing off

SESSION SEVEN: PAGES 150–72

RELAXATION SESSION: BREATHING AND FEELING ♥

EXCHANGING A WHOLE-BODY MASSAGE
Beginning the massage
The legs
Working up the torso
The arms
The shoulders and chest

THE THREE KEYS:
MOTIVATION, BREATHING AND POSTURE

Before moving on to the sessions, a brief examination of these three key topics may be helpful. It is helpful to make a habit of briefly checking them whenever you are about to begin a session of relaxation or massage. You may come to find it a useful habit in other situations as well. The more you are able to bring your intentional practice of relaxation into every facet of your life, the more healing relaxation will be.

MOTIVATION

Whenever we set out to do anything in our lives, the motivation is the key governing factor which determines the result. This is true of all activity, from the most trivial to the most profound. To take an example of the first kind: what motivates us to put on certain clothing when we get up in the morning? Do we put on a uniform which is required by the institution with which we are connected? Do we choose something which makes us look sexually attractive, thus earning the admiration of some and jealousy of others; or something which helps us to disappear and not be noticed at all? Is it simply a matter of wearing clothes which feel comfortable, or those which look good in the mirror? In fact, what exactly (climate aside), motivates us to get dressed every morning at all?

Day after day, week after week, the motivation for the way we dress, however unconscious, will affect the way we feel about ourselves and how others see us. If we dress with the motivation to benefit ourselves and others as much as possible, then the choice of clothing will be a positive matter for us. For one person this might manifest as fashionable dress with a positive wish to please all onlookers and attract compatible friends. For someone else, choice of clothing may be a major form of self-expression or even a means of self-healing through the use of colours which help to balance personal weaknesses. For another, it might mean wearing one or two simple garments, depending on the weather, with the intention not to get involved in the game of display and attraction and to use money in ways that seem more beneficial. Whatever the inner logic, a strong positive intent gives meaning and value to the business of wearing clothes.

When it comes to learning to relax, our motivation will also largely determine the result. If we want to get rid of aching shoulder muscles or insomnia without having to use drugs, this is already a beneficial intention towards ourselves. If we want to help family members to relax by learning simple massage, this reflects a good motivation towards those close to us. If we are, however, willing to engage the reality of the suffering of all living beings, and, deep within our hearts, we have the wish to help them, then we are on the way to developing universal compassion. Whatever efforts we then make to benefit ourselves and others will tend to be increasingly effective.

However, along with the wish to benefit everyone equally, we need to learn to let go of expectations. When we begin working, no matter how positive the motivation, we may not be capable of helping very much at all. We may find that our efforts to help bring no apparent results and after a few sessions we might feel like giving up even on being able to help ourselves. So isn't it rather unrealistic, presumptuous even, to think about helping all living beings? Not if we are able to let go of our own expectations and work with a truly open mind. Then we will be less inclined to shut out opportunities to be of benefit. However, we also need to be content to start from where we find ourselves right now. If getting rid of our own headache or helping our child to sleep is all we can take on at present, then this is our starting point for the practice of universal compassion. Tomorrow may be a different story; a little patience is required.

Within the following sessions, whether in a group or on your own, it is recommended that you take time at the start of each exercise to consider your motivation for what you are about to begin. Why are you here, and for whose benefit exactly? Start with the simple facts, even if they seem quite negative. Maybe a friend brought you along and you didn't know how to say no. Then see if you can find in your heart a simple wish to get the most out of it for yourself, at the same time as pleasing and supporting your friend. Then, as much as you feel able, allow the field of benefit to expand as far as you can.

When it comes to massage it is very important to check your motivation before you touch your partner. It is important to let go of your own worries and preoccupations, and especially anything you might want from the other person. Make a simple wish that you may be able to help the other person to relax and to feel well in him- or herself.

If possible, imagine that there are lots of other people receiving a massage at the same time and wish that they all receive the benefit. This last thought may help you to avoid the expectation of producing results. With the kind of massage being taught in this course, you are not aiming to treat illnesses or injuries, but rather to help create the conditions, through relaxation, where healing can take place. If one were to think of adopting a role, it would be more that of a servant than of a doctor, though the attitude of a humble friend comes even closer.

For all the exercises in this book, it would be beneficial therefore to reflect on your motivation for the work you are about to undertake.

BREATHING

Breathing is a symptom of being alive. It continues whether we are aware of it or not. So why should we be concerned about breathing? Breath is a linking factor between our mind and our body. The way we breathe affects the way we think and feel; and the way we think and feel affects the way we breathe. By becoming aware of the breath in a simple, non-interfering way, we can greatly increase our ability to help ourselves. Although the normal breathing pattern of each person is unique, many people breathe in an unbalanced way which contributes to physical and mental suffering. When we relax we 'breathe easy' and our whole system is suffused with oxygen. It is also fed at a more subtle level with prana, chi, ki, energy or endorphins, depending on whatever system of interpretation and explanation you wish to follow. For the purposes of this book, however, it doesn't matter what it is called, only that we come to be able to recognise the sense of greater aliveness that accompanies easy breathing.

As a general rule, to breathe less is to feel less. Many people habitually hold their breath as a way of keeping feelings hidden. This pattern may well develop in childhood when we judge, consciously or otherwise, that it is not safe for our feelings to be known to others. From this strategy of suppression we can easily begin to lose touch with our own true feelings. If you have adopted this strategy in the past, it takes some courage to embark on the path of deeper breathing and feeling. It is not possible to change the pattern of a lifetime overnight, nor is it wise to try. But as with all real inner change it can only begin with awareness. Once we notice that we are using only a fraction of our breathing capacity, especially in tense or potentially emotional situations, then little by little our willingness to breathe and to feel will increase.

Others have the habit of over-breathing, taking gulps or gasps of air into the region of the solar plexus with a lateral movement of the lower rib cage and with a tense throat. This tends to increase mental agitation and emotional reactivity. As with under-breathing, the first step to revising this pattern is to become aware of it. Once its effect is witnessed and understood, it will gradually resolve itself. How can this be? Because there is an instinctive intelligence in our mind that relates to the needs of the body. If we do not override it with thought or unconscious, negative patterning, it will inform and advise us as to what is needed to restore our balance. For example, when we are thirsty and drink, we don't need to think about it. However, if we suppress the natural impulse to drink, this can lead to dehydration and various health problems. So it is with breathing. When we learn to be aware of our breathing pattern without interfering with it, it will gradually right itself.

Similarly, if you are working at your office desk and you hear two colleagues talking in an argumentative way which gives rise to anxiety in you, you may hold your breath to control the anxiety. However, if you are in the habit of noticing your breath, this suppression will feel silly and you will easily resume breathing, without 'doing' anything. In the breathing exercises given in Session One (pages 34–35), we will learn to open up to a fuller and easier pattern of breath.

Breathing is also important in the practice of massage. If your breathing is smooth, slow, and open, it will help you to stay open to your partner, whether you are giving or receiving the massage. Sometimes, as beginners in giving massage, we feel that we don't know what we're doing at a certain point. We might even panic. However, if we check the breath, taking a few slow inhalations and exhaling fully and completely, the feeling for what we are doing may well return. Recalling the motivation, the simple wish to help the other person to relax, helps the breath to come naturally. It can also help us to know how the other person is feeling to follow their breathing pattern for a minute or two. Further, by breathing fully, it is also possible to help our partner to remember to breathe.

POSTURE

Posture is also a very important element in both self-healing and the skilful practice of massage. Without changing anything, notice the way you are sitting or lying right now. Notice the position of your spine. Is it straight or is it slumped forward or bent to one side? In general, when the spine is straight, but relaxed, the body has the fullest opportunity to restore itself in rest and be able to express itself in movement. A straight spine keeps all the nerve pathways as open as possible, so helping the mind to remain clear and fresh.

However, a straight spine does not mean a rigid one. Very often when the topic of posture is raised in a group, some people will suddenly straighten up from a slumped position, but in a very rigid and unnatural way. This is often a reflex action left over from school years when children were punished for bad posture. The military model – chest up, shoulders back and stomach pulled in tight – was the ideal put forward. However, this model fails to teach awareness of the subtler feelings of the upright spine, the sense that it grows from the root of the coccyx, stabilises its base in the broad sacrum, and grows upward with a lifting movement as a blade of grass is drawn up to the sun.

Again the question of motivation arises: motivation towards yourself. If I am out to criticise, punish and correct my bad posture, I will prefer the military approach. However, if my motive is to discover and unfold a healthier pattern for my life, I will prefer a gentler model. In either case, it can be seen that the potential to sit or stand up straight is a privilege and one that can be lost to any of us at any time. So clearly a habit of slumping or of sitting or standing in an unbalanced way can gradually rob us of the privilege of an erect spine as surely as can a serious accident or a disease.

Posture is also important in the practice of massage, as a balanced and free feeling in one's own body readily communicates itself to someone else. When giving massage it is important to be ready to shift your posture and position as often as necessary in order to remain relaxed, well-balanced, and with as straight a spine as possible. A twisted posture can easily lead to an uncomfortable feeling for the person giving the massage which is likely to be communicated to the person receiving it.

Awareness of posture, like that of breathing, is something that develops best when it is cultivated consistently over a long period of time without too much intensity of effort. Under these conditions, lifelong attention to posture can bring benefits to health, outlook and appearance right through to old age.

MASSAGE

The approach to massage presented here is based on the premise that the potential to help yourself and others through touch is part of being human. If you have hands and good will and a bit of patience you may well be able to benefit another person through massage the very first time you try it. In fact, even monkeys pass the time exchanging something like massage, so it is hardly a subject that you have to go to school to learn. For many people the main thing to be learned is how to overcome a shyness associated with touching other human beings. Loss of confidence in instinctual knowledge is also an obstacle. What makes us look in books to find out about massage also sends us to the library or the specialist to find out how to give birth, enjoy sex, prepare food and a myriad other things that our ancestors knew either by instinct or through learning from their elders. That said, there are some very useful books on massage a few of which are listed at the end of this guide. For this reason I have made no attempt here to write a complete introduction to the subject. Rather, I want to encourage people to get started by experience, by feel alone, and to find out more about massage in whatever way is most appropriate, and in their own good time.

In the last 15 years or so, with the boom in alternative medicine, literally hundreds of massage techniques have appeared under different names in Britain and North America alone. Most of these techniques have a name and an expensive training course attached to them. I personally question the motive behind this diversification. On the whole, we learn what will be helpful to others by experiencing it ourselves and once that experience is integrated, it becomes ours to share wherever it might be beneficial. Each person has their own natural rhythm and style of massage just as each of us has an individual style of handwriting. By receiving massages from different people we can expand our repertoire of techniques. But a compassionate motivation towards the other, and trust in our own instinct for what to do next, remain the most important qualifications.

When I first came in contact with massage, as an exchange student in Pakistan thirty years ago, it was a wholly new experience and a very positive one. It was part of the daily routine of my host family in Karachi for the daughters to massage the legs of their elders every afternoon and then to exchange massage with one another. When I returned to America a few months later, there was simply no context for what I had learned: massage was still a dirty word. Since then, however, massage has become more and more acceptable to ordinary people as a way of reducing stress and helping with various conditions such as headaches, back pain, rheumatic pain, premenstrual tension and other common complaints. It is also recognised by some as a constructive way to share time with friends.

There is, however, a widespread lack of experience of wholesome touching in many post-industrial cultures, and those adults who cannot remember being touched in a kind but ordinary manner may find it difficult to share their good intentions towards friends and family in this way. Indeed, the very idea of massage can have risqué connotations for those who remember touching entering their lives only at the time of their first sexual experiences. And when these memories are unhappy ones, attitudes are likely to be even more confused and ambivalent. So learning to give and receive massage which is relaxing and beneficial can be problematic for some people. Massage should never be imposed upon anyone because someone else thinks it would do them good. In fact, the basic rule for all massage, whatever the context, is that 'the customer is always right'.

In this approach to massage there is no need for people to remove clothing. Whether it is comfortable and appropriate to do so depends on several factors: the temperature of the room, the culture, and the sense of personal security of the participants. My own experience is that unless both giver and receiver feel comfortable about the removal of clothing, nothing is gained. The massage begins on a false basis where one person is trying to be more open than they feel, and the other is trying to make up the difference. This is not relaxing. It is always possible to accommodate your technique to clothing – even an overcoat if necessary.

In giving massage, it is also important to acknowledge your own boundaries. If you offer someone a massage and they strip off completely without invitation, in a way which makes you feel uncomfortable, it is best to express your unease. Better still, you might suggest how much clothing you feel it is necessary for someone to remove before any misunderstanding can arise in the first place. In the context of a 'beginning to relax' class, this would most often just be bulky or hard outer clothing such as jackets, belts and shoes.

Contra-indications for massage

There are certain situations where it can be dangerous to apply massage so common sense is always required. From time to time a person's reaction to massage may be ambivalent or even negative. In this case, you should stop and discuss what the cause could be and only resume if you both feel confident. Or you may have a feeling that what you are doing doesn't seem beneficial, but you don't know why. This may not necessarily be simply a feeling of nervousness or doubt on the part of one or both parties, but something stronger perhaps, even an intuitive feeling of doing harm.

For example, once I was massaging the legs of a lady in her early sixties. She complained of a very painful calf muscle in one leg. I set out to massage gently, but was confused because she had not engaged in any exercise and had no pain at all in the other leg. (She was also feeling and acting quite dull and uneasy.) So I stopped the massage and asked her to see her doctor right away, just to be sure there was no chance of a blood clot in the leg. The next time she came, three weeks later, she reported that there had indeed been a clot in a deep vein and that the doctor had told her that massage might have sent the clot to the lungs via the heart. Stopping the massage was based more on an intuitive feeling that all was not well than on any specific knowledge of symptoms. In general, therefore, if you are clear in your intention only to benefit and never to do harm, such rare but potentially dangerous situations can be avoided.

In addition to these general guidelines, there are a few specific contra-indications for massage which should be studied and taken to heart:

* Do not massage varicose veins on or near the area of the swelling except with the gentlest stroking in the direction of the heart.

* In pregnancy, do not use pressure-point massage as there are certain points that might tend to cause a miscarriage. In the first three months it is best to massage only on the advice of a physician, and only gently thereafter until the baby is due. Many women in labour find that massage is very helpful for relaxation and the easing of lower back pain.

* Do not massage a person who has suffered a heart attack, or who you know or suspect has a history of high blood pressure, except on the advice of a physician.

* Do not massage when a person is suffering a fever.

* Do not massage in the area of any red, hot, or unexplained swelling.

* When a person is known to have cancer it is best not to massage without the advice of a physician as there is thought to be a small chance that massage could spread cancer cells to other parts of the body. In cases where the cancer is already spread throughout the body, massage can be very helpful for relaxation

and to counteract the common experience of loathing for the diseased body.

* Strong pressure-point massage should not be used on young children or very elderly people. In both cases the physical system is very sensitive and force is not necessary.

* Wherever there is a known injury or strong pain do not massage until the person has first received medical attention and advice.

* Where there is a history of epilepsy or acute nervous disorders, it is best not to massage the head. It is also better practice in such cases to massage down the body, from head to toe, rather than in the opposite direction.

* As with all rules there are the exceptions which can be discovered and used as you develop in experience, knowledge and skill. Further hints and personal observations about massage will be mentioned during the sessions.

GROUP WORK

There follows a few suggestions for those who undertake this work in a group. For the meeting place to be appropriate it should be large enough for everyone to lie down and the floor space should be clean. It must be warm and free of draughts, but not airless. If possible, it should be fairly quiet and free of outside distractions and the possibility of interruptions. Since some people may only feel comfortable undertaking this work if they know they are free to come and go, while others may feel insecure unless the group is quite stable, it is important for all participants to maintain an open and liberal attitude, and to be mindful of the needs of the others. As long as each person remembers that they are present first to learn to relax themselves and second to learn to help others to relax, then all should go well. The work is probably most beneficial if no individual assumes the role of leader, but rather everyone agrees to learn together, even if some people are more experienced at the outset. However, it could be useful for a different member of the group to take charge of each session, especially as regards going over the instructions for the exercises and reading out the methods of relaxation and visualisations for the others to follow.

If you feel you would like to undertake this work in a group, but feel you need some help to get started, you may contact any of the Tara Rokpa therapists, trainees or helpers mentioned at the end of this book.

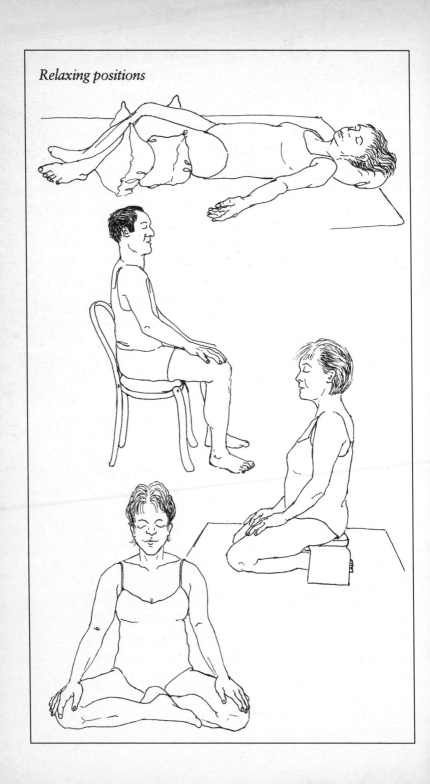

Relaxing positions

Session One

Breathing is the first of many relaxation exercises which can be done alone or in a group. These exercises can be practised either lying down, on the back, or in a sitting position. Many people, at least in the beginning, find it more relaxing to practise lying down comfortably, but not on a sagging mattress nor a cold hard floor. In this case, there should be some support for the head, so that the neck is slightly extended and the chin tucked in a little. The legs should be extended and with feet together. If there is any discomfort in the lower back, put cushions under the knees, or even rest the legs on the seat of a chair. If your clothing is tight enough to notice, loosen it. And be sure that you are warm – with padding underneath and, if necessary, a cover over you. Find your best position, and relax into it. Take the force of gravity as your friend and simply let go.

If you are sitting in a chair, check that your feet are flat on the floor and parallel, with your spine straight, lifting up from the seat, like a blade of grass growing towards the sun. If you are sitting on the floor, be sure that you are seated on cushions that are high enough and firm enough so that you can balance without putting a strain on your lower back. It is recommended that both knees rest on something padded. Or you may prefer to kneel, with the help of a meditation stool. In either case, there should be no strain involved in keeping your back straight. Feel that your chest is very open, but not braced, and that your shoulders simply hang like a coat on a coat hanger. Your head should be tilted slightly forward with a feeling of being lifted by an invisible thread at the centre point of the rear fontanelle, or crown. Alternatively, it may be helpful to feel that your head is balanced effortlessly like a ball on a long pole. Your hands can rest gently together in your lap, palms upward, or palms down on your knees. Again, find your balance and relax into it.

Whether lying or sitting it is better to allow your mouth to rest slightly open, with the tongue gently resting on the hard palate just behind the front teeth, so you can breathe through the mouth and nose together. If this does not feel comfortable, however, breathe in whatever way is easiest for you.

Basic breathing exercise ♥

Now focus on the feeling of your body as a whole. Feel the weight of your body and be aware of the sensation of pressure at various points where your body makes contact with floor or cushions. Relax into the feeling of heaviness, just letting go and trusting the force of gravity to keep your body still and stable. Be aware of the right and left sides of your body, and of an imaginary centre line from top to bottom, making sure that you are resting in a symmetrical position. Feel that from this centre line everything on the right falls away to the right and everything on the left, in its turn, settles to the left.

Now notice that despite of the stillness of your body, nevertheless there is movement; most noticeably the movement of the breath. Simply rest and be aware of the sensations of movement within your body.

Now focus particularly on breathing in and breathing out. Notice the sensations of the air entering your body, through the nose and mouth, following the feeling of the air moving down the throat and into the lungs and out again. Without doing anything special with your breath, just notice these sensations of the air coming in and going out.

Now be aware of your lower abdomen and notice that at the start of every in-breath, your lower belly rises, and with every out-breath it falls. If you have any doubt about this, rest your hands lightly on your abdomen just below the navel. While continuing to breathe normally, follow the up and down movement of your lower abdomen.

If you are not used to this kind of exercise, you may find it difficult, at first, to breathe normally while observing the movement of the breath in this way. Just be patient with yourself and don't make too much effort. Check to be sure you are not tensing any muscles unnecessarily. There is no need to hold your stomach in, or to clench your jaws or tense pelvic muscles. See if you can let go a little more with each out-breath. Just let the breath flow smoothly and evenly of its own accord.

Now to deepen the relaxation of the breath, breathe in a little more slowly and deeply than usual, counting slowly as you breathe in, until your lungs are quite full, but not uncomfortably so. Next, hold your breath to the same count. Then exhale through your mouth, quite forcefully and completely, while imagining at the same time that you are emptying out a glass of dirty water. Feel that you are able to let go of any pain, tension, worries; in fact anything that you don't need. Repeat this sequence of inhaling, holding and releasing three times.

Now return to the natural pattern of the breath, watching in a relaxed way, as though waiting and watching for wild animals in the forest, patiently and with a gentle, relaxed concentration. If your watching is too intense the animals will feel it and stay away. It is similar with the breath; its natural pattern will only be seen if you are able to observe lightly, almost casually.

Follow the sensations of each breath entering your body, then let your mind go free with each out-breath. Bring your attention back to the in-breath at the very moment that the breath turns round and the air starts coming inside. Whenever your mind wanders, which it will naturally do, gently bring it back as soon as you notice. You can skip the scathing comments. Losing attention is normal and inevitable so it's important to learn to notice that it happens without getting upset about it. Just like a child learning to read, working through mistakes is a critical part of the learning process.

Continue this for as long as feels natural, but not for more than ten minutes or so to begin with. When you end the exercise, let both your awareness and bodily movement come back slowly, in their own good time.

If at any stage during this or any of the exercises which follow you feel uncomfortable, or under pressure, remember that your mind is your own and just relax as best you can, in your own way.

WARMING-UP ♥

Hand warm-ups are a sequence of exercises for waking up, loosening up, sensitising and strengthening the hands and wrists. Not only are your hands the main tools for the practice of massage, they also allow you to communicate with others through gesture and touch, and to express yourself through play, work, and creative action. To feel helpless and useless is to feel handless, in some sense.

When our energies are blocked, we don't feel we can make contact with others. We may feel tense and at the same time exhausted or depressed. The hand warm-up exercises can be useful for all of these situations, as well as for preparing for a session of massage. Although these and all the exercises which follow are gentle, and are meant to be done in a relaxed way which should cause no harm, everybody is different. So, if for any reason you feel uncomfortable in carrying out an exercise, or if you should feel any sharp pain, then leave that exercise alone, at least until you can understand the source of the discomfort.

SHOULDERS AND ARMS

Our hands hang off our arms, which hang off our shoulders, so to relax the hands, the shoulders must first be released.

Shrug and relax
Stand with your feet apart and body straight. Slowly breathe into the lower abdomen and gradually shrug your shoulders right up to your ears. Hold for a few seconds, then drop your shoulders, exhaling forcefully and completely through the mouth at the same time. Repeat several times.

Folded-arms circles
Fold your arms in front of you. Now roll them up and away from you, then down and back towards your chest in a full circle a few times, consciously stretching and opening the area between the shoulder blades on each circle.

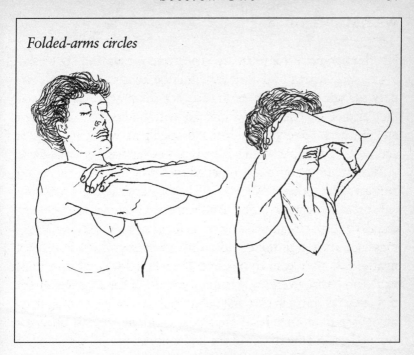

Folded-arms circles

Repeat, this time circling your folded arms in the opposite direction, rolling them back towards you, close to the chest and down, then up and around again. Try to feel that you are bringing the inner tips of the shoulder blades together on each roll. Now keeping the arms folded as before, circle around in a big circle to the right a few times, and repeat circling a few times to the left. Be sure to keep breathing fully throughout this exercise.

Finger-linked ceiling stretch
Interlock the fingers of both hands and extend them fully in front of you with the palms pressing out (see illustration overleaf). Now slowly stand on tiptoes while moving your extended arms up until your palms face the ceiling, while slowly inhaling at the same time. Stretch as fully as possible. Now, while slowly exhaling, let yourself down from tiptoes, at the same time letting your interlocked hands float down, turning naturally until they rest folded at the level of the navel. Now gently reverse your hands so that the interlocked fingers are pressing forward as before.

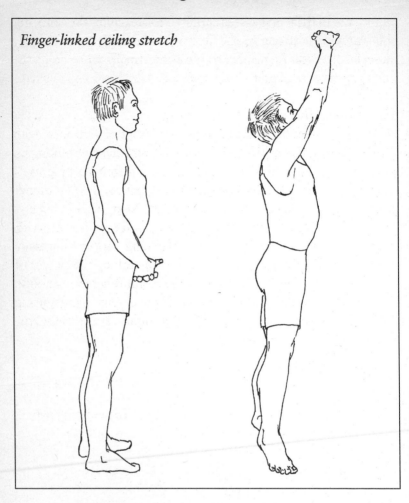

Finger-linked ceiling stretch

If at first you find it difficult to balance standing on your toes, you can still do the exercise standing normally, but stretching as fully as possible to the ceiling, and then bending your knees a bit as you bring your hands down and exhale. Repeat this a few times.

WRISTS

Strong and flexible wrists allow energy to flow more easily into the hands. The following are two wrist stretches that I first learned in aikido, the martial arts system notable for teaching the 'unbend-able arm', made strong by the flow of vital energy rather than by muscular strength. Remember to breathe normally while doing the following exercises, and to keep your shoulders loose and relaxed.

The jumping fish ★

Hold your left hand about 20 cm (8 in) in front of your face, with your fingers straight and together, palm facing you and pointing up to the ceiling. Now press the four flattened fingers and palms of your right hand horizontally across the left, with your right thumb pressing against the back of your left hand. Next, make a big arc, in a motion like a fish jumping, leading with your left wrist, extending your left arm up and over, stretching back the fingers of your left hand with the right, but especially taking the power of the stretch in the left wrist. Repeat this several times in a smooth, long arc, stretching but not straining. Now change hands, using the left hand to assist the stretch of the right; repeat the whole sequence three or more times.

The jumping fish

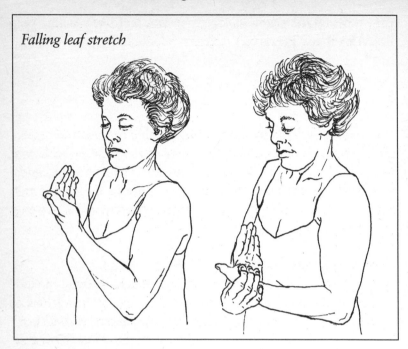

Falling leaf stretch

Falling leaf stretch ★

With a relaxed stretch, reach with your left arm above your head
with your palm and fingers facing forwards. Now allow your hand
to drift downwards, spiralling inwards like a leaf falling from a
tree in autumn. When it reaches the level of your heart, wrap the
fingers of your right hand around the base of your left thumb.
Now press your right thumb into the back of your left hand below
the little finger. Then, continuing the spiral motion, use your right
hand to help the twisting of the left, drawing the left wrist down to
the level of the navel. Hold it there for one slow cycle of in-breath
and out-breath. Repeat several times and then repeat the whole
cycle several times, beginning with your right hand above your
head.

Hand flapping

Hold your hands hanging loosely at chest height, about half to a
full arm's length in front of you. Now shake your hands vigorously
at the wrists, flapping them as fast as you can for as long as you

can, moving your arms as much as you feel like. Again, keep breathing freely. This is very effective in loosening up stiff wrists.

HANDS

Your hands are equally gifted in being able to send and receive information. To practise massage properly you must exercise both functions. You need to be able to sense and feel with your hands, and then to respond. Flexibility is also important and, to a certain extent, muscular strength. The following exercises aim to develop all these qualities.

Exploring hands

Starting with your palms together, lightly touching, sense the feelings of your hands when they are still. First feel the sensations of your right hand beginning with the fingertips, and travel with your mind down through your hand and wrist to the elbow. Now shift your attention to the left hand and scan your sensations in a similar way. Next use your two hands to explore the full range of movement of each joint, rotating, gripping, and bending forward and back. Notice carefully what degree of stretching feels beneficial before it becomes too painful. Your own limits become the rough guide in working with others. Let your two hands play together, exploring the strength and flexibility of each finger as well as that of each hand. The habit of playing with your hands like this can be relaxing in itself, as well as useful for learning massage.

Raising and sensing warmth in the hands

We are often unaware of warmth in our bodies unless we are too hot or too cold. Yet body warmth is one of the defining characteristics of being alive. We eat food for fuel and this is burned in the metabolic process to produce energy for activity, from the most subtle to the most gross, as well as to generate warmth. Energy is a word that can be used in many ways, some more precise and meaningful than others. While human life is clearly more than just a physical process, and there are subtler energy fields to consider, we cannot hope to benefit others at these levels until we have thoroughly understood them within ourselves. This understanding only comes through direct experience stabilised through extensive and intensive practice.

In the world of massage I have been exposed to many theories and many treatments supposedly based on knowledge of subtle energy. I'm not sure I have benefited from any of them, but I am quite sure I have suffered needlessly from some. That said, I do believe it is important to feel for yourself that some energy is really 'there', whether we consciously exploit it or not.

So, first rub your palms together lightly, but very rapidly, keeping the hands as relaxed as possible. When both hands feel very hot, slowly and gently separate the two palms, sensing the relative warmth and coolness each hand picks up from the other at different distances. Continue this for a few minutes, sometimes bringing the palms as close together as you can without physically touching, and then exploring sensations in both hands as you play with the space between them.

SELF-MASSAGE OF THE SHOULDERS, ARMS AND HANDS ♥

Self-massage is a discipline in its own right. At the same time it is a natural progression from the kind of explorations already described. It also provides the most reliable field for experimentation in learning to work with others. As we will see in various relaxation and visualisation exercises, our ability to feel for others in a genuine sense, begins with being able to experience our own needs accurately and compassionately. As we become more effective in using our hands to benefit ourselves, we will naturally have more knowledge, and thus more confidence, to do the same for others.

There is a very thorough system of self-massage from which I have learned a great deal. It is called *do-in*, and is Japanese in origin. This system, presented in several books in English, gives many well-illustrated exercises and techniques far beyond the scope of this guide. For those who are interested, it is also a way to become acquainted with the acupuncture meridian system, which forms the basis of theory and practice for many Oriental massage and medical traditions.

Self-massage of the shoulders, arms and hands, as briefly presented here, is an extension of the hand warm-ups, and may be included in a longer session focused mainly on yourself, or used as needed (or as time allows) in preparation for a session of massage with a partner.

SHOULDERS AND ARMS

Whenever you are massaging a part of the body that is large enough to accommodate your whole hand, it generally feels best to get acquainted by beginning with long, smooth strokes. At this stage, whether the subject is yourself or somebody else, you are using your hands to investigate what you are feeling. At the deepest level you will notice where there is bone close to the surface, where there is hard muscle, and the temperature and texture of the skin where you are touching it directly. As far as possible, let your hands do the thinking. Work through the following exercises with one hand and then repeat on the other side, using the other hand.

If you have long fingernails, you may notice that you cannot apply pressure freely with your fingertips and thumb without hurting yourself. Although it may seem a big sacrifice, if you are interested in learning to practise massage effectively with others, or even for yourself, it is important to keep your nails trimmed short.

Shoulder to chest stroke
Begin by placing your right hand over the muscles between your neck and your left shoulder. Press firmly with your palm and all your fingers. Now dragging your fingers forward over your shoulder, complete a long stroke with the flat of your hand down to the centre of your chest. Repeat a few times.

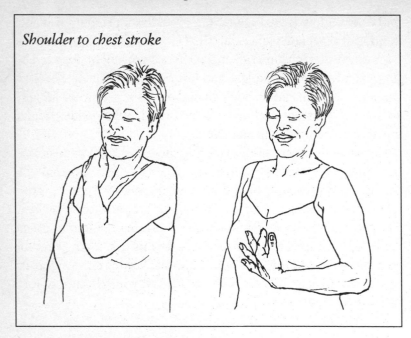

Shoulder to chest stroke

Kneading the shoulder muscles

Using the thumb and fingers, but mostly the fingers, of your right hand, knead the muscles and flesh between your left shoulder and neck. If the muscles are very stiff and tight, you may want to increase the pressure in order to try to loosen the muscles. If these are very sore, however, experiment using lighter pressure, since it is difficult to let go while experiencing pain.

Warming the shoulders

Using the fingertips of your right hand, feel into the indentations and soft spots around the shoulder joint. Gently rotate your shoulder into different positions and notice points that may be a little sore to press, but where it also feels relieving to do so. Now, with a relaxed palm, rub round and round the shoulder until you can feel some warmth. Simply hold your hand there, especially over any sore point.

Warming the arms

With a relaxed open palm, first rub your left upper arm briskly up and down. Now knead the muscles and flesh, using your whole hand, but especially squeezing the flesh of the left arm between your fingers and the mound at the base of your right thumb. Use fingers and thumb to explore and locate sensitive spots. Through cautious experimentation you will find points which, while initially sensitive to pressure, feel better quite quickly with gentle circular movement and moderate pressure.

Continue down the arm, exploring the elbow with your fingertips. Squeeze and press the forearm, as above. You may find you can use the pad of your thumb more easily here for applying pressure to points along the bone on top of the arm and into the wrist. Always begin with gentle to moderate pressure to points and then increase it if it feels right. Particularly do this if you are proud of your physical strength and like to approach things in a vigorous way. It is important to learn to approach first yourself, then others, with a gentle awareness.

HANDS

By now you have already practised many of the elements of hand massage during the exploring and stretching. However, it is worth mentioning at this point that there are several systems of pressure-point massage which seem especially effective when applied to the hands and feet. One system is known as zone therapy, and another as reflexology, which has various branches. Another, similar to *do-in*, is known as shiatsu and this, in turn, is quite similar to acupressure. While each of these methods has something unique to teach us, they all assert that pressure applied to points of the hands and feet are effective in releasing tension and blockages in other parts of the body as well.

It is all too easy for people with little or no medical knowledge to begin diagnosing their own and others' ills by finding sore points on hands and feet and then matching them with points on a chart relating to one of the systems of pressure-point massage. If you study all the charts you will see that there are many different designations for the points. So it is probably better not to play this game. At best it distracts you from learning to feel things directly, while at worst it can cause unnecessary worry about health, or even delay a person from seeking professional health care where such is needed. If through your reading and experience you find you have a special affinity with a particular system, you may wish to study and train to the point where your skills in diagnostics and treatment are recognised by those qualified in the particular method. However, this is way beyond the scope of what you might learn from this book.

Massaging your own hands gives you the chance to explore and increase your sensitivity in finding effective points, and in learning to apply pressure appropriately. The points that feel good to you are likely to be helpful to others as well. In the beginning therefore, before studying any system, it is useful to learn to massage your hands as thoroughly as you can.

Exploring fingers

Starting with the thumb, grasp the end of each of the fingers of the left hand in turn at the corners of the nail. Squeeze firmly between thumb and forefinger and move on to the next. Grasping the whole end joint of each finger in turn, pull and stretch firmly but don't jerk. Using thumb and forefinger, explore each finger, searching out sensitive points. Wherever you find one, maintain a tolerable degree of pressure through either pressing, pressing and releasing, or circling on the point, until the pain becomes less. This lessening of sensitivity usually takes just a few seconds and not longer than a minute. Where the level of pain does not decrease within sixty seconds, either the blockage is persistent and deep-seated or there is another cause not susceptible to relief through massage. As always, it is important to use common sense here and lighten up where there is sharp pain or pain that feels 'wrong'. Be sure to carry out this investigation as thoroughly as you can. Repeat for the other hand.

The palm

In massaging the palm of the left hand, you may use the base of the thumb, thumb pad and tip, and fingers of the right hand. It is good to experiment with different strokes: pressing and holding, pressing and releasing, light stroking and circling, and deep stroking and circling. The guidelines for knowing how long to stay with one spot are the same as above. Repeat for the other hand.

The back of the hand

The back of the hand has less flesh and muscle than the palm, so in general you will want to use less pressure as you seek out the sensitive points which lie under the skin along the bones. It is also important, here as elsewhere, to watch out for distended or broken blood vessels. Particularly in older people whose skin is fine and papery, it is best to use minimum pressure, especially in areas where blood vessels are clearly exposed. Massage both hands equally in the time available.

Linked hands: thumb to palm pressure

To reduce the amount of strength needed to thoroughly apply pressure to points on the palm, link fingers of both hands loosely and press with the thumb of one hand the palm of the other. By

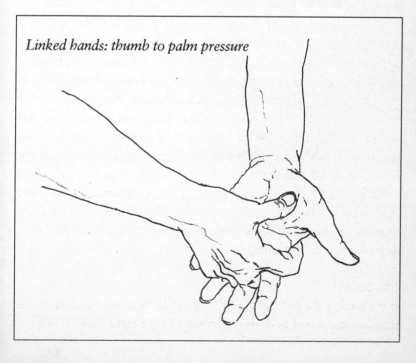

Linked hands: thumb to palm pressure

combining the muscular strength of right and left arms, firm pressure can be simply applied with minimal strain.

GROUP WORK

The friendliness exercise given below allows you to explore further the dual function of your hands as transmitters and receivers of vital information to and from other people. This can be tried with as few as two, but better with four or more people in pairs. It is little known that it is at least as difficult to receive a massage properly as to give one. To get the most from massage it is necessary to trust and open up to what the other person has to give without trying to protect yourself or control the situation. This exercise has two purposes: first, to appreciate the unique quality of each person's presence and each person's touch; and second, to practise taking turns in being the one who initiates and leads for both, and being the one who follows the lead of the other. Or, to use the language of the exercise, to take turns being the 'driver' and the 'passenger'.

Friendliness exercise
Very occasionally, due to arthritis in the shoulder, this exercise could be uncomfortable. If this is the case it is as always best to leave it out.

Begin by standing in pairs facing one another. Join palms so that the palms and fingers of both your hands are touching those of your partner, with shoulders dropped and relaxed at a distance which is comfortable for both.

Decide, within each pair, who will first be the 'driver' and who the 'passenger'. Allow yourselves to stand for a few moments simply being aware of your own sensations and feelings, and your feelings in relation to your partner. If you are feeling at all nervous or uncomfortable, see if you can open up a bit just to acknowledge your partner as a unique human being with his or her own feelings, experiences and patterns, and as a potential friend. It is not necessary to maintain eye contact unless it is comfortable for both

Friendliness exercise

partners to do so. Indeed, some people may find it easier to relax by closing their eyes for part of the exercise.

Now as driver, begin to circle your right hand and arm in a clockwise direction. Circle smoothly in a way you feel will give a nice ride to your passenger. As passenger, simply go along for the ride without trying to take control of the wheel or trying to put on the brakes. For some people this is very difficult and yet the cause of the difficulty may be entirely unconscious. So if your passenger

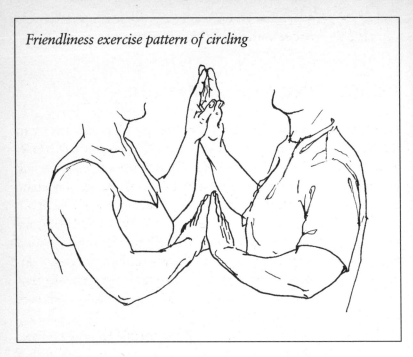

Friendliness exercise pattern of circling

is taking over without seeming to notice it, as driver stop circling so your partner can feel this for him/herself. If you as passenger feel uncertain or confused as to whether you are doing it right, just take a few deep and easy breaths and let go as much as you can. All you have to do is follow. When it feels quite smooth and easy, the driver can stop circling with the right arm, and begin circling, once again in a clockwise direction, with the left. Repeat the same procedure.

Sometimes people find their arms and shoulders begin to ache while doing the exercise. This is probably due to tension which was already there. It may also be due to inequality of height. In either case, first do some exercises to loosen up the shoulders. Then experiment with distance to be sure it is as comfortable as possible for both of you. Above all keep breathing fully.

Now reverse roles with the 'driver' becoming the 'passenger' and the original 'passenger' leading clockwise circles first with the right arm and then with the left. Once there is some feeling of meeting and moving together smoothly, then each person should find a new partner. If the group is large enough, each person could complete the exercise with three different partners.

EXCHANGING A HAND MASSAGE

Hand massage is one of the easiest to share with people in day to day life. Children enjoy it and will want to give you one too. It goes very well at a hospital bedside or just when a friend is feeling low and needs to relax. It is important to know, though, that some people experience hand massage as very intimate and it is therefore a way to get close to someone very quickly. By remembering the importance of the clear motivation you will be able to deal with a person's discomfort, even rejection, with skill and humour. An important part of learning the skill of massage is remembering that you are wishing to help, but if you cannot, by working with care you can be sure there is no harm.

Through the self-massage of hands and the friendliness exercise, you will be well-prepared for exchanging hand massage with a partner. You will already have some idea of what feels good and effective through your experience of massaging your own hands. In the friendliness exercise you will have had some practice of giving and letting go.

In fact, there is very little instruction needed for hand massage. It can be undertaken with both partners seated in chairs, both seated comfortably on the floor, or with the person receiving the massage lying down, with the partner who is offering the massage seated alongside. There is no one right way, but it is important that both people should be comfortable and that the person giving the massage should be prepared to move as often as necessary, while the receiver rests undisturbed. The person receiving the hand massage should not have to hold his/her hand up to make it accessible. So it may be useful for the arm to be supported with a cushion at the elbow or resting in some other way.

It is very important to massage both hands equally and only fair that both partners have a nearly equal opportunity to give and receive the hand massage. It can be helpful for one person to take the

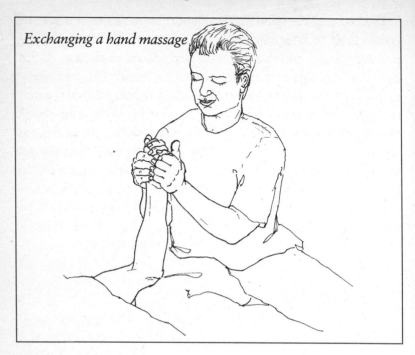

Exchanging a hand massage

role of timekeeper for the group so you can divide the allotted time four ways. Five minutes is really the minimum needed for each hand.

As discussed in massaging our own hands, if there is a lot of tension in the shoulders, it is difficult for the hands to let go. So, beginning with your partner's right arm, check for tension in the shoulder. This is easily done by very gently swinging the arm by the hand like a rope. If there is no swing, cradle the shoulder with your left hand, while supporting the weight of the arm with your right hand and forearm, loosening it as best you can.

It is not generally useful to make your partner self-conscious either about his/her muscular tension or breathing. However, if the breath is being held, then you could breathe deeply and audibly yourself. If the release of the shoulder does not happen, just let it be. Make some contact, firmly squeezing down the arm from the shoulder to the wrist and then proceed with the hand massage. The more tense your partner is at the outset, the more patient and open you need to be. If you can find and keep the simple motive of friendliness, relaxation will follow.

Proceed with the hand massage, your partner's elbow supported comfortably by floor, knee or cushion. Begin just holding the hand, making contact, and then let your hands do the exploring, the discovering. Investigate whatever you feel you would like someone to do for you. Try different degrees of pressure and ask your partner to let you know if anything doesn't feel right. With some people this could be if the massage was too strong while for others if it was too light and 'tickly'. Don't be afraid to pause any time you feel you are getting lost or confused. Simply check your breathing, your motivation and your posture and then proceed – listening with your hands. When you have finished the right hand, move round to the other side and massage the left. Then change roles, so each of you gives and receives a complete hand massage.

Session Two

We have already briefly explored the meaning and importance of breathing and of developing awareness of the breath. Before proceeding with the next set of exercises, we will consider the word 'feeling'. In English we use the verb to feel in several different ways. It refers to the experience of a vast array of physical sensations. We feel sensations of contact with such external phenomena as rain, wind, fire, ice, rock, silk, porridge, plastic, etc. We feel with our hands, both passively and intentionally, but we also feel with our whole bodies, picking up information about the environment with every changing sensation. Other people and animals appear before us, make sounds that we may hear, or touch us, and again this gives rise to a variety of physical sensations. The experience of such sensations is, however, highly subjective. For example, one person may find the sensation of touching velvet very agreeable, while another may find it disturbing. So whether we feel something as pleasant, unpleasant or neutral will vary considerably according to the individual and the particular situation.

We also feel physical sensations that are entirely internal, such as the feelings of the breath coming in and out of the body. Other feelings arise relating to the circulation, digestion, body movement, nerve activity, and so on. Some of these sensations can be extremely subtle and fleeting and often it is difficult to name them or even be sure that they really do exist. Again, these sensations may be experienced as pleasant, unpleasant or neutral.

We also talk about feelings in the emotional sense of the word. We feel happy, sad, angry, affectionate, helpless, confused, or whatever. And these emotional feelings are often associated with physical sensations, whether consciously or otherwise. We might, for example, breathe fast and tense up when afraid or, conversely, first notice a pain in the stomach and only later realise that we were angry about something. So it can be helpful to pay attention to such links between physical and emotional feelings. Not cutting off one from the other can be an important key to relaxation and self-healing.

Feeling can refer to intuition or instinct, as in 'I have a feeling...'. This type of feeling may also have a component of physical sensation, albeit a subtle one.

As regards our feelings towards others, various considerations apply, but there is no denying that our awareness of and reaction to other people and animals can have a powerful effect on our experience – just as we, in turn, affect others. Not that it's always easy to express these feelings in words. For example we might say we like or love someone when what we mean is they make us feel good in some way, inspiring sensations or emotions which, on the whole, we find pleasant. Someone we don't like, on the other hand, might give us, or indeed be a pain in the neck. We might call this type of feeling the feeling *of* another person, although in many cases such feelings are readily changeable. Then there is another type of feeling that we might call the feeling *for* another, which is not so changeable. It is the capacity to feel empathy and true concern for others, which does not depend on feeling better or worse ourselves. This feeling for the other is the basis of true compassion.

The second part of this exercise is really a natural continuation of the first. The subtle level of awareness you have been cultivating allows you to notice more and more detail of sensation at every stage of each breath. Proprioception is the faculty that enables us to feel sensations within our own bodies. Just as we can learn to see more and more accurately by training the faculty of sight, we can also learn to feel more and more precisely by training the 'proprioceptive' faculty.

In this exercise you will be doing primary research or investigation into the field of your own sensations. It is a little like looking at a drop of pond water. With the naked eye you might, at most, see a wriggley speck. With low magnification you can see there are several living beings and some debris. With increased magnification you may make the acquaintance of strange and remarkable creatures you never imagined were there. If you don't take the trouble to be very still and look in a careful and steady way, you will never see any of this. And if you get excited about the new friends in the drop of water, you will lose the ability to observe accurately at all. This is also the case when observing bodily sensations. While your body remains still, your mind will be alert, but also steady and relaxed. You are not making anything up, or even doing so much as trying to relax, you are simply noting and observing, through the faculty of proprioception, exactly what you are feeling at each moment as you bring your attention to bear on a specific part of the body.

Breathing exercise ♥
Begin the second session by reviewing the previous instructions for the breathing exercise on pages 34–35. Follow this exercise as before, but with the following variation for deepening the relaxation.

Instead of taking three deep breaths and holding them, take twenty-one breaths that are only slightly slower and deeper than your normal breaths. Pause for a moment or two at the end of each exhalation and each inhalation, counting each cycle of exhalation, pause, inhalation, pause, as one breath. As in the first version, visualise that with each out-breath you are emptying a glass of dirty water which carries away with it any sort of pain, tension, irritation, or anything you don't need.

Now return to the natural pattern of the breath, according to the previous description on page 35.

Feeling exercise ♥
Begin by gently moving your attention from awareness of the sensations related to the breath, down to sensations in your feet. Try to observe the feelings which arise on both sides of the body at once without trying to make them match up, but rather just noticing what is there which is the same on both sides as well as anything which seems different.

Bring your attention down into the big toes of both feet. Notice whatever sensations you may find there, without judgement or comment as to light or strong, good or bad. Do you notice any warmth? any coolness? any tingling? any pain? Even if you feel nothing at all, simply be aware of whatever arises and then allow your attention to move on to the second toes on both feet and along, one by one, to the little toes. Then allow your attention to move gently up the feet in a similar way.

Continue slowly and carefully up through the ankles, the lower legs, the knees, the upper legs and hips. When you come to an area where there is pain, or even the memory of pain, try not to get involved in stories of how it happened, or speculation about what might be causing it. Try to maintain a slow, steady flow of attention where you are gradually moving your consciousness up through the body, investigating sensations with an increasingly detailed awareness, while at the same time not getting caught up or bogged down in any particular area, or set of sensations. It is something like entering a flower garden where the more still and open your mind, the more you notice and the more free you are to appreciate what you see.

When you have completed your exploration of the hips, move your attention to your hands, and beginning with the thumbs, travel with your awareness through each of the fingers of both hands. Then continue in the same fashion up the hands, wrists, forearms, elbows, upper arms and into the shoulders. At some point you may come to an area that feels 'dead' or blocked in a way that is difficult to move through. Do not try to force anything. As with any particularly strong or dynamic sensations, it is best not to give these experiences special importance. Rather try to keep a very open and steady mind – not judging anything – but gently returning your attention to the task of observing sensations in the very moment they are happening, letting go of all other possible projects and preoccupations for the duration of the exercise.

Next move your attention to the base of your spine, to the tip of the coccyx, and move very slowly up the spine, vertebra by vertebra, taking note of all the sensations throughout the torso and at the level of the vertebra you are focusing on at the time. So first feel the sensations in the lower pelvic area, without trying to identify what sensation is coming from where. Then continue up the lumbar and lower abdominal area, then up through the waist, and so on. When you reach the upper vertebrae, at the level where the neck begins, feel the sensations inside the throat, moving up under the tongue, then feeling the lower jaw, the inside of the mouth and the place where the spine fits into the base of the skull. Then continue up the head and face, feeling the surface sensations as well as those which can be felt deep inside the head. Bring your attention to rest at the point at the top and centre of your head.

Now reverse the direction of the flow of attention from top to bottom. This time you will be exploring whole fields of sensation, rather than examining the body part by part. It may help to imagine that your body is hollow and upright and filled with water, and that the plug has just been pulled from the bottom. What you then follow is a moving slice of sensations as the water level slowly moves down the body. In any case, regarding the body as a whole and, starting at the top of your head, allow your awareness to move down steadily, but rather more swiftly, through the feelings at each level. Down through the head and face and throat and neck. Then down the shoulders and chest, upper back, upper arms, midriff, through the waist and elbows, hips, upper legs and forearms, wrists and hands, and on down the legs through the knees to the feet. When you reach the feet once more, try again to sense what is happening in each toe. You may well find that your ability to feel sensations, especially very subtle sensations, in detail, has improved.

To end the session, simply feel your body as a whole. Open up completely to whatever thoughts and feelings may arise, just letting them come and go freely without any restriction or interpretation. When you feel ready, stretch your body very completely and, in your own time, sit up.

In the beginning especially, people experience this exercise very differently. At the extremes there are people who say they feel nothing and others who feel so much that they are unable to bear it. In the first case it is good to come back to the more obvious sensations like the feeling of pressure in contact with the floor and of the abdomen rising and falling. Then gradually, if there is no panic or effort to feel something more or different, the ability to be aware of other, subtler sensations will increase.

In the second instance, where there is too much feeling, it is important to proceed slowly and do short sessions, focusing on slow and even respiration whenever too much fear or excitement arises. It may also help to try the exercise sitting rather than lying down. Some people find that after doing the first part of the exercise, when the awareness moves up the body, they are left with a giddy, unbalanced feeling as though there is too much happening in the head. If you have this experience, then always practise the feeling exercise from head to toe. You can do it in great detail first and more generally the second time, but it should reduce the experience of having too much energy trapped in the head.

The importance of this exercise cannot be emphasised too strongly. Staying in touch with ourselves at this level is the basis of self-knowledge and self-healing. Many of us have been conditioned, or have conditioned ourselves, to block out or deny the experience of sensations in the body, because it is easier or more convenient not to have to deal with them. For example in school we learn to suppress the need to go to the toilet until official break times in order to avoid the embarrassment of asking permission. This may lead to a life-long habit of ignoring the sensations which tell us it is time to go. Similarly, we may be frightened of the consequences of feeling anger or desire. So rather than learning to face and deal with these feelings, we tend to ignore or deny the physical signals that tell us what we really feel. We may also have a fear of doctors or of ill-health, and rather than face the problem, we may practise denial of the very sensations which might tell us about those changes in our bodies that need attention.

Trying to live our lives authentically and fully without awareness of what we are feeling in our bodies is like trying to write a book without knowing the alphabet. By being able, through the faculty of proprioception, to pay attention to whatever feelings may arise, helps us to overcome fears about the physical body. By staying in touch with ourselves at this simple level, we are able to tell the difference between normal changes which come and go, and conditions that could develop and grow worse and which require expert advice. We can also grow wiser in regard to ourselves by seeing the links between physical states and emotions we would rather not know about. We cannot investigate the emotion behind clenched jaws until we can feel the physical sensations caused by the action.

Following sensations in this way is also naturally absorbing and thus naturally relaxing. As with observing any other natural phenomenon, like a river or a rose, or the wind in the trees, following the flow of bodily sensations is relaxing in itself. The ability to feel what is going on within ourselves, without reacting, is the basis of self-acceptance.

ROOTEDNESS AND SLOW WALKING ♥ ★

The rootedness exercise below helps us to explore our relationship to the earth. When we walk from place to place we do not float like the moon walkers; rather we plant each foot, in turn, on the earth in accordance with the force of gravity. Our unique physical structure as human beings allows us to stand and walk upright. The physical co-ordination of our bony skeleton is connected by joints, held in ever-changing place by millions of muscle fibres, which receive instructions through countless nerve pathways emanating from the central nervous system. As babies, we instinctively use our legs to kick and push; while as toddlers, still very close to the ground, we learn to walk, with many little falls as part of the process. If we watch infants learning to walk it is amazing how quickly they establish the ability to balance on two small feet. The ground and what is happening on it is still the child's main reference point when out of the mother's arms, and in spite of the newness of the child's movement, there is something incredibly stable about it. There is a rooted quality, like a well-planted young tree. Even when the child falls, if the parents don't fuss, the toddler re-establishes contact between feet and earth and is up and running again. Often we lose this rooted quality through the way we use our bodies and minds. Our relation to the earth as our support and the force of gravity as our life-long challenge becomes distorted. The rootedness exercise may help.

The two exercises that follow, practised separately or in succession, can serve as effective antidotes to the speedy, distracted, unearthed qualities of modern life. They can help to strengthen the stability of the earth element within us, without losing the moving and uplifting quality which comes through the air element. Once the sequence is natural and familiar to you, it can be a very practical tool in daily life.

For example, imagine yourself in a giant shopping mall a few days before Christmas. There is Christmas muzak piped from every direction, competing with a Salvation Army band downstairs and a band of choristers from the local school upstairs. There are hordes of shoppers all desperately wanting to fulfil some inner longing by the purchase of objects for those they love, or owe, or wish to impress. Every shop is decorated with tinsel and flashing fairy lights. Most of the items for sale have been picked over and are not where they are supposed to be. The gaily dressed shop assistants all have the same glazed over look in their eyes. Small children are looking for Santa and bursting into tears when they find he was here yesterday. By now you have forgotten what you were looking for and your mind is completely swamped with confusion at all that is for sale. If you simply stop where you are and re-establish contact with the earth, feeling your feet take root, you may be able to avoid panic and despair. You may also be able to walk slowly and consciously to the shop you need or else out through the nearest exit.

Rootedness exercise

Stand with your feet about the width of your shoulders apart, toes pointing forward. (You will find this exercise easier if you try it barefoot or in socks or slippers.) Focus your attention on your feet, feeling the sensations of contact between your feet and the floor, or ground, on which you stand. Experiment by subtly shifting your weight to the balls of the feet and back to the heels, and from the outer edges to the insides. Keep the movement and variation minimal, but notice the differences in how your feet feel, how your ankles, knees and hips feel. Also experiment with the bend of your knees. See how it feels when your knees are locked straight, and the feeling when there is a half-sitting angle. Then try the positions in between until you find the most balanced and comfortable position of all.

Next imagine, as you gently shift your weight, that you are growing roots from your heels and then from your toes. Feel that a whole network of fine roots is growing deeper and deeper down into the earth. Feel the stability of your roots and then, slowly and gently, put it to the test by moving your body in all the ways you can discover without lifting your feet entirely from the ground. Let your body twist and swing and sway like the branches of a tree in a high wind, all the time keeping your sense of rootedness.

Slow walking

Now very slowly shift your entire weight on to your right foot, conscious of the root system which grows from your heels and toes, spreading wide and deep beneath your feet. Then imagine that your left foot is magically freed of its roots and acquires a small bunch of helium balloons attached to its top which lifts it slowly and effortlessly up in a high, floating step. Then carefully step down onto this same left foot, conscious of the sensations of making contact with the ground once again. Now slowly shift all of your weight on to the left foot and feel it taking root.

This time imagine your right foot freed of its roots and lifted by a bunch of balloons. Walk in this way, as slowly as you can for at least a few minutes, placing full attention on the different phases of walking. Use it as a chance to explore the alternating feelings of heaviness and stability in stepping down on the earth, with the feelings of lightness and buoyancy in lifting the foot up. You might try inhaling each time you lift your foot and exhaling each time you place it on the ground. Walking, when moving like this in slow motion, conscious of all the associated feelings, becomes very smooth and easy. It is not necessary to exaggerate the floating step once you have the rhythm of it. Gradually increase the pace without losing awareness of any of the sensations of walking.

WARMING-UP

Go back to Session One and repeat as many of the exercises for the shoulders and arms and wrists as you feel necessary (pages 36–41).

SELF-MASSAGE OF THE FEET ♥

Self-massage of the feet follows much the same pattern as for the hands, however this may not be quite so obvious if you have not tried it before. First you need to find a comfortable position for holding and applying pressure to one of your feet at a time. If you are accustomed to sitting cross-legged on a cushion on the floor, this position works well. Otherwise you may want to lean against a wall for support, with the leg you are not massaging stretched out in front of you; or you can sit in a chair with one leg crossed over the opposite knee. However, if you are not feeling well or are very tired, you might prefer to lounge back against several large pillows so that your whole body and head are supported in a semi-reclining position. Then with one knee bent to support the other crossed over, you may well be able to reach and hold your raised foot while comfortably resting your shoulders, head, neck and back. Whichever way you sit, try to keep your back and shoulders as relaxed as possible while using your hands to make the acquaintance of, and apply pressure to, your feet.

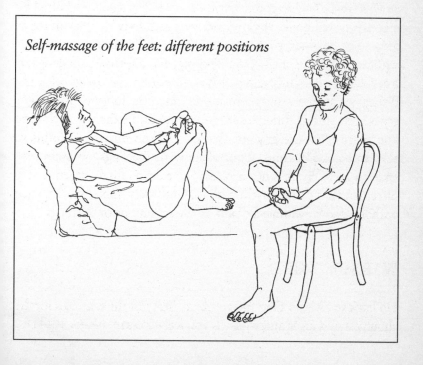

Self-massage of the feet: different positions

Foot massage

To prepare the foot for massage it is helpful to loosen it up by grasping just above the ankle with both hands and shaking very rapidly, so the foot flaps, as in the wrist-flapping exercise in Session One. And, as with the hand massage, you will want to explore the range of movement and stretch in the ankle, foot and toes. Allow time for this, as most of us are much less familiar with our feet than we are with our hands. The great advantage you have in massaging your foot is that you have two free hands available so make full use of them. Experiment with different ways of holding your foot in both hands, as this enveloping contact feels very good.

Go back to the step-by-step instructions and advice for massaging your hands (pages 45–48) and apply them here. The main emphasis should be on thoroughness of exploration. Slow down and really feel what is going on. You will probably find that you can use more pressure on the sole of your foot than felt comfortable on the palm of your hand, but there is no need to strain yourself.

Pay special attention to the points along the inside of the foot, starting at the inside of the big toe and continuing along the bony ridge of the instep to the inside of the heel. According to reflexology, these points are especially effective for the spine when the pressure is strong. Following the same line, when the touch is light and feathery, it is extremely relaxing for the whole body. Little children will often quickly go to sleep through the influence of this light massage, but you have to catch them first!

You will also want to explore points at the back of the heel, along the Achilles' tendon, and all around the ankle. On top of the foot, from behind the toes, trace upward between the tendons.

If you find this form of massage makes you feel better, as many people do, you will probably want to investigate foot reflexology. There are many useful books on the subject, some of which are mentioned in the bibliography. However, there's no need to hurry. The more you discover for yourself first, the less likely you will be to dwell on the menu at the expense of the meal.

When you have finished massaging one foot, take time to note the difference in feeling between the two feet. Exercise your proprioceptive sense for a moment and see what can be felt in each of your feet. Try standing up. You may well find that one foot feels warm, open, relaxed and awake while the other feels relatively dead. Now go on and massage your other foot.

You may be aware by now that your feet have been somewhat neglected. They are miraculously powerful components of the human body which normally bear much of the load of a human lifetime – with very little recognition or appreciation in return. Many people feel ashamed of their feet, particularly when the shoes and socks are removed. Getting into the habit of massaging your feet regularly, using a little oil or lotion, is a way of helping to relax and balance your whole physical system while at the same time taking care of those unsung parts which carry you and connect you to the earth. In my opinion, this does not need to be a solemn or serious business. If you are in the habit of watching television as a way of relaxing at the end of the day, try massaging your feet at the same time. In this way your hands will grow stronger and more skilled and it will be rather more beneficial than just watching television. For a special treat, try soaking your feet in hot water with a few drops of peppermint or lavender essential oil before the massage. This will soften them up and help the oil or lotion to penetrate hard skin. Caring for your feet in this way, you may become aware that you could use the attention of a chiropodist to cut funny toe-nails or remove corns and calluses. You may also notice that your shoes are not so good for your feet and feel that it is time to look for footwear that gives a bit more support. Learn to value and care for these loyal friends. They will thank you many times over in the years to come.

If you practice self-massage of your feet regularly, you will discover that it is one of the most effective tools for self-healing and for relaxation.

Session Three

This chapter begins by looking at the first of the visualisation exercises that are presented in this book. Many people think visualisation is something very complicated. In fact, the mind's ability to create pictures and images within itself is very ordinary and something we do all the time without instruction. For example, do not the words Mickey Mouse conjure up some fleeting image in your mind? The visualisations given in *Healing Relaxation* all have self-healing as their aim. By intentionally calling up very pure and beautiful images in the mind's eye, it is possible to increase the tendency towards positive change within the body, the emotions and the mind.

The most common problem people have with visualisation is that they may try too hard to create a solid picture. However, it is in the very nature of this kind of seeing that it is transparent, and not solid. Further, clarity is not enhanced by trying harder, with a more intense level of concentration. A more supple and relaxed mind seems to help. Each of the visualisations presented here use immediate, present experience as its basis. The felt sensations of the physical body, the moods and emotions, and mental states as we experience them, provide the raw material for positive transformation through the visualisation of pure colours. While the colours are by no means arbitrary, the meanings and values given here are not the only ones possible. However, it is important to have full confidence in what is being visualised at the time, rather than casting about for other possibilities. Once any particular session is ended, it is quite possible to practise some other visualisation which gives different significance to the same colours.

The feeling exercise on page 56, which gives us an intimate acquaintance with, and easy access to, the sensations of the physical body, is the best preparation for these visualisations. It is also helpful to check your motivation quite clearly at the start of any session of self-healing visualisation. Without trying to force any-thing, it is important that you sincerely wish to be free of pain, anger, fear or whatever you might be trying to improve through visualisation. Indeed, the depth and whole-heartedness of this wish may be the strongest factor in determining the effectiveness of any particular session. It is helpful always to wish the best for all others too, and to take special care not intentionally to exclude anyone from your good wishes. This provides an open ground for self-improvement, while beginning to extend the benefit further afield.

The White Light Visualisation is the first of three exercises that follow the same pattern. The white light relates especially to the healing of the physical body, the red light relates especially to healing emotional pain and blocks to expression, while the blue light concentrates especially on healing fear and anxiety and mental disturbances of all kind. Each of the three lights can carry out the work of the other two; there is no rigid separation. However, it seems useful to many people to focus on these three areas of difficulty one at a time.

The frame for each of these visualisation exercises is a com-pletely open sky in which appears the sphere of the five pure elements, represented by five rainbow colours of light. This is a symbolic expression of the dynamic balance that exists between the elements which make up the whole of this Universe, including the planet Earth and our own human bodies. The rainbow sphere appears as a radiant sphere made of five jewel-like hues: golden yellow light (the essence of earth), radiant diamond white light (the essence of water), ruby-red light (the essence of fire), emerald green light (the essence of air), and deep blue light (the essence of space).

Even though all five colours are equally represented, their distri-bution within the sphere is constantly changing like the colours on a soap bubble, becoming more intensely vivid and clear. The sig-nificance of this very beautiful appearance is its purity and completeness, the very essence of all that is beneficial and whole-some is included here. Nothing is missing. There are many aspects to be explored and discovered in relation to the elements, but this is not the purpose of this particular visualisation. If you would like to pursue these ideas further see *Working with the Elements*, a paper I wrote for Tara Rokpa in 1993. However, in each of the three visualisation exercises given here, all five of the pure elements as expressed through the five colours, dissolve with all of their qualities and powers into one single colour. The white sphere of light, for example, no longer has any special relationship to the water element. Now it is the quintessence of all five elements dissolved into the one form most suitable and appropriate for healing the physical body.

Different people have widely diverse experiences of visualisation and none is right or wrong necessarily. Further, the same exercise practised ten times by the same person will always be different. There are some types of visualisation that supply a great deal of detail about what you will see or experience. This visualisation and the others to be given here are of another type. Only the simplest description is specified in terms of colours of lights, their locations, their meanings and their effects. Everything else you will 'see' depends very much on your own experience and how your mind works.

For this reason it is advisable not to compare your own experiences with others who are just beginning, but rather to learn to accept and work with whatever comes to you. If you do feel the need to discuss your experiences, it is probably better to talk to someone who has worked with these exercises over a long period of time. Or if you don't know of anyone, then write to one of the Tara Rokpa therapists mentioned at the end of this guide.

BENEFITS OF THE WHITE LIGHT EXERCISE

Very often when we are physically ill we feel helpless about what we can do about it. Even if the cost and availability of medical attention are not an issue, we may still feel confused about what type of medicine we need. Then, when side effects of treatment arise we may wonder whether the doctor knows best. If it seems a minor problem there is the thought just to leave it alone and do nothing. But what if it gets worse? If it is a life-threatening condition, fear and anxiety about illness, treatment, loved ones and responsibilities we are not able to fulfil, and ultimately, about death, can torment us far more than the disease.

The white light visualisation exercise gives us a way of improving the conditions for healing whatever the circumstances may be. Some people have the experience that their pain becomes less through the influence of the white light visualisation. Others notice that they are less anxious and more relaxed, so both illness and treatment are easier to take. Others find that their illness becomes the occasion for being able to recognise the sufferings of others which in the healthy state are easier to ignore. This may increase their capacity for appreciating others and understanding better what we all have in common. This empathy becomes the basis for deep compassion.

As with the other exercises given in this book, once they become very familiar we make them our own. At this point, like a good companion, we can take them anywhere and relate to them informally as well as formally. A doctor's surgery waiting room is a great place for practising a short version of this exercise. Or how about when you are waiting in a queue and you sneeze and feel you might be coming down with a cold? The white light is a universal healing friend, always there when brought to mind.

To help work through the visualisations included in this book, memorise the stages of the exercises or if you are in a group situation, one person might read out the instructions. As a third alternative, cassettes containing all the relaxation exercises described in this handbook are available by post from Tara Rokpa, Edinburgh (see useful addresses).

THE WHITE LIGHT VISUALISATION ♥

Begin the exercise by finding a relaxing position, lying or sitting, and allowing your body and mind to settle naturally. Now use one of the two exercises from the previous sessions for deepening the relaxation of the breath. Then return to the natural pattern of the breath, simply noting the sensations of the breath coming into the body, allowing the mind to relax with each out-breath. Now that you have had some experience of going into the sensations of the body in this way, your faculty of proprioception will be more easily awakened. As soon as you feel able to pay attention to the sensations without too much distraction, allow your awareness to travel throughout your body, scanning all the different sensations that may be found there.

You may follow the methodical pattern of the feeling exercise, or you may proceed in a freer way, but do try to include all areas of the body in your investigation. You might imagine yourself in a low-flying airplane, making a survey of features of the land below. Only in this case you will be noting warmth, pain, vibration, pressure and so on, instead of rivers, hills and trees. At least ten minutes will be needed for this settling-in part of the exercise, but you might need considerably more time to feel that you are in touch with what is going on at all levels of sensation within your body.

Practising the visualisation

Imagine in front of you a completely open sky as seen from a high place; either a perfectly clear and cloudless blue daytime sky, or a night sky filled with millions of stars. First simply relax your mind, looking into the open space.

Now a pin-point of light begins to come towards you from the centre of space. As it draws nearer, you can see clearly that it is made up of five rainbow colours, expressing the power and quality of the five elements in their most essential form, as light. Each is very pure, brilliant, and intense:

* Earth, with its essential qualities of stability and heaviness in the form of golden yellow light.

* Water, with its essential qualities of wetness, cohesion and flow, in the form of brilliant diamond white light.

* Fire, with its essential qualities of reactivity, illumination and warmth, in the form of brilliant ruby-red light.

* Air, with its essential qualities of movement and intelligence, in the form of brilliant emerald green light.

* Space, with its essential qualities of openness and limitlessness, in
  the form of intense deep blue light.

As you imagine the sphere of the elements before you, all five
colours constantly moving and changing but always in balance,
always in harmony, you feel that all of the healing power in the
Universe is available to you here in the very beautiful appearance
of the rainbow sphere.

Now you see all five of the colours with all their qualities and
powers as the essential form of the elements, dissolving into the
single diamond white light.

The sphere of brilliant white light you see in front of you in
space has a special ability to heal the physical body. Imagine the
white light comes streaming towards you and enters your body
through a point in the centre of the forehead. It travels freely
throughout your body bringing feelings of lightness and relaxation. Wherever the light contacts areas of pain, tension or disease,
there is a sense of improvement. The residue of this healing
process, the pain, tension, discomfort or disease, which is stirred
up through contact with the white light, then leaves the body with
the out-breath in the symbolic form of thick black smoke. When
the smoke leaves the body with the out-breath it disappears about
30 cm (12 in) away from you, so there is no question of its pollut-
ing the environment.

If for some reason you find it difficult to imagine the light
coming into your body through the forehead, then you may
imagine it entering with the in-breath and spreading through
your body. Or you may imagine that it comes like a gentle
shower raining pure white light which enters everywhere without
resistance.

Whichever way you visualise this process, the result is the same.
The radiant white, healing light, which contains the pure essence
of all the elements, spreads relief from physical suffering and all its
causes throughout the body. As the residue of this process continues to be expelled with the out-breath, the whole body gradually
grows lighter, less and less solid, and the smoke you breathe out
becomes less and less dense. Little by little, it feels as though your

whole body is composed of pure white light. At this point your out-breath becomes the same as the pure white light which you take in. Continue this process until you feel it is complete or, if you find it hard to relate to at first, until you have had enough.

If you feel you have received some benefit from the practice, then think of others who have a great deal of pain or other physical suffering. Imagine that the light also goes out to them and they are helped by it.

Now the rays of light that have been going out towards you and others are gradually reabsorbed into the sphere of pure white light before you in space. At this stage, the white sphere changes back into the sphere of the elements with the five colours again sparkling before you in all their clarity and intensity. As you look at this very lovely appearance, you are aware that it is something you can bring to mind for your own benefit and the benefit of others whenever you want or need to. Now the sphere moves away from you in space, until it disappears. Allow your mind to rest completely. When you are ready, stretch your body thoroughly and sit up.

LIMP

Limp is a game for two. As far as I know it was invented by my sister and me when we were six and nine years old respectively. As I recall it was my first link with conscious relaxation and it was fun. It is a light-hearted way of checking, and then extending, your ability to let go in the hands of another human being.

When playing this game in a group, or with someone you don't know very well, it is important to be aware that for some people, letting go of control of the body may feel threatening, if not impossible. As in all other aspects of this work it is essential to remember that no one should be forced or pressurised to participate in anything that does not feel right for them. Facing refusal or rejection from a would-be partner is also an important part of learning to relax. It is equally important to be able to say 'no' if you don't feel right about participating. Learning to play these various and progressive roles with increasing confidence and humour is a rewarding aspect of the work. Limp can be played as often and for as long as you like. Children love it. After all, they invented it!

The game of Limp ★

As partner A, lie down on the floor on your back, with arms and legs extended, and let go as much as possible. It helps to think of yourself as a life-sized rag doll with no control over your own limbs. They can move, but only when someone else moves them.

As partner B, you may rearrange, rotate, lift, swing, shake, shift, flex, or whatever any part of A's body in any way you like, as long as it's done in a way which you are sure can do no harm. For example, raising your partner's leg 60 cm (2 ft) off a thick mattress and dropping it, is within the rules of the game. Dropping it from the same height on to the bare floor is not.

Your aim as partner A is to maintain the state of a rag doll, making no movements of your own and offering no muscular resistance, as long as your partner plays fair and causes you no pain.

Your aim as partner B is to catch A out so that some resistance to movement occurs, or some movement is initiated by A and not by you.

As soon as B catches A either initiating or resisting movement, then the roles change and B lies down and plays the rag doll.

In the beginning, it is better if B is quite tolerant of resistance to, or initiation of, movement by A otherwise, in many cases, the game will never get going. However, since it is very relaxing and enjoyable to have one's limbs moved harmlessly about, many people increasingly learn to let go. This is very good training for massage in both roles, as we begin to experience first-hand the rewards of relaxation as well as the obstacles to it. In a playful way we learn how important trust is. We learn how to handle the various limbs of another person's body with both ease and due respect. We may also learn how to communicate non-verbally our own trustworthiness. This largely depends on being able to pick up the messages given by the recipient of our care.

EXCHANGING A FOOT MASSAGE

As with any session of exchanging massage, it is good to notice how much time you and your partner have to spend between you, and then agree how that time will be divided. Half an hour is really about the minimum time possible for an exchange, as this allows less than 10 minutes for each foot. A full hour for both of you is more realistic.

A short session of preparation (reviewing motivation, breathing, posture, and a short session of hand warm-ups – see pages 36–41) should be done by the person offering the massage. The one receiving might check for clean feet, and then get comfortable, breathing easily.

It is the responsibility of the person giving the massage to check that their partner is going to be comfortable, especially warm enough. Lying relaxed for more than ten minutes it is easy to get chilled, so depending on the climate, it is wise to have a light blanket to hand. Once your partner is settled comfortably, you should be the one to do whatever moving is necessary. The person receiving the massage should be free to be as close to a 'rag doll' as possible. So be prepared to change the position of your chair or seat so that you may have best access to one foot or both.

There are several possible positions for giving and receiving foot massage, so you may like to experiment from among the following options:

* Both partners sit in chairs placed at right angles, so that the person receiving the massage places one foot at a time in the lap of the other. Try to find a way of partially supporting the leg at the same time, so there is not undue strain on the knee in the fully extended position. A large cushion in the lap may help.

* The partner offering massage sits on the floor cross-legged, or leans against a wall with legs outstretched. The partner receiving lies comfortably on his or her back on the floor, placing one foot at a time in the lap of the other. Various angles for sitting and lying are possible, but you are looking for the position that is

Positions for exchanging a foot massage

comfortable for both of you. It is generally good to look for a position that leaves as much space and freedom of movement as possible. Taking two feet into your lap close into the abdomen might seem quite cosy at first, but it may well feel too close and cramped after a short while. Making contact from more or less a right angle, one foot at a time, is usually most spacious.

* The partner receiving massage may lie face down on a mat or blankets on the floor, with a soft cushion under the chest so there is no strain on the neck when the head is turned to one side. The person offering massage can then easily sit to one side, bending the partner's leg at the knee, making the foot available at such different heights and angles as are convenient. This last method gives the person offering the massage the most flexibility, but has the disadvantage that it is difficult to observe the partner's facial expressions, which often give the most immediate feedback as to the effectiveness of the work.

* It is possible to work with the person receiving the massage lying on his or her back on a massage table, with the giver seated in a chair at the foot of the table.

Giving a foot massage

Many people believe their feet to be especially ticklish, so it is helpful to start the massage just holding the whole foot quite firmly. In fact, it feels best to make contact with both hands to both feet at the start of the massage and at the end. Never be afraid simply to leave your hands where they are for a minute or two. This allows the partner to get used to having his or her feet touched. It gives you time to check the three keys described on pages 20–26 before you begin again.

Whenever you initiate a new move it is good to make contact smoothly and gently but firmly, maintaining continuity of contact wherever possible. As with the hands, the amount of pressure that feels good will vary significantly from person to person, so you must be ready to alter your technique depending on the feedback you receive. If you have been practising self-massage on your feet, you will have enough to go on regarding the basics of giving foot massage to another person.

The best advice I can offer is practice, practice and more practice. As you gather more experience, you will also gain confidence in being able to offer foot massage to people in various situations without feeling embarrassed about it. It is good to practise not taking it personally when someone declines your offer of massage and at the same time not letting it deter you from offering another time. At some stage you will know that foot massage as you are practising it is effective for relaxation, and perhaps helpful in other ways besides. That is the stage at which reading and further training can be very interesting and useful.

Session Four

The point in time when our ancestors decided to get around on two legs rather than four was not a good moment for the human back. Indeed, this particular evolutionary development placed essentially unnatural strains on the engineering of the human body from which subsequent generations of human backs have never recovered. When we used our arms as front legs the load on the spine was evenly spread, stress upon and compression of the lower back far less pronounced. Nowadays our work, and even many leisure activities, compound that stress and compression, giving rise to a variety of problems that do nothing to enhance the quality of life. So, at this stage it might be an idea to spend some time simply crawling around on your hands and knees. Do your back a favour; rewind the evolutionary 'tape' back to your animal days.

If you are uninhibited enough to try this either in your relaxation group or at home, be sure you have a carpet or blanket on the floor, or you might find any gain for the back is paid for with sore knees. Feel how natural and comfortable it is to move around like this, with the forces of gravity more evenly distributed, the strain and pressure reduced on a variety of moving parts. It can also be beneficial to come into closer contact with the earth. Our hopes and fears, thoughts and dreams are often far removed from the ground, the working basis, the reality of our condition.

Many of our back problems would greatly be eased if we spent more time on the floor – not just sitting or lying there, but moving around, stretching, exploring movement. Whenever the back feels tired or painful during study, work or socialising, while standing or seated on chairs, it is always worth considering moving your activity to ground level where you have a greater range of possible positions. Getting up and down from the floor helps maintain overall co-ordination and flexibility especially in the legs. Obviously there are many situations where this would be socially unacceptable or where the floor is too hard, cold or dirty. But if you feel it is helpful, there is no reason why you can't make certain parts of your home comfortable and clean for 'floor-living'. Even people with healthy backs might find a little daily floor-time beneficial, whether alone or among close friends.

The final introductory point is that a common cause of lower back and hip complaints is the cold climate in many countries. So it's important, especially during seasonal changes, to keep warm. Keep, and particularly sleep, out of draughts. Wear a long sweater or body warmer, wrap a shawl around your waist, but anyway keep your lower back comfortably warm.

BREATHING AND FEELING ♥

By now the breathing and feeling exercises described earlier in Sessions One and Two should be familiar, and as with many such activities, you may well find that they are now coming more easily and their effectiveness has improved with practice. So start Session Four with Breathing and Feeling, as before (pages 56–60), allowing as much time as is necessary to achieve a relaxed, aware and comfortable state. As mentioned in Session Two, some people find that moving the awareness up through the body can lead to a spaced-out, or fuzzy and unbalanced feeling in the head. This could be due to an imbalance of the air element, which can generally be avoided by working in a head to toe direction. In such cases, this is recommended.

GROUP WORK

The exercise described here, as presented by Akong Rinpoche, is designed to help us overcome any fear of what is behind our backs, unknown and unseen, and to develop a measure of trust and confidence. This exercise finds its fullest expression when conducted in a standing position. If your partner is much taller or shorter than you are, or if either of you have some kind of weakness in the knees or lower back, then a simplified, sitting version is fine. The exercise consists of a spontaneous exchange of movement, rather than a choreographed set-piece.

It can be very enjoyable and, like the friendliness exercise, goes well if you are working in a group. So, according to the time available, a session might involve trying the exercise with three different people. In this way, you can realise how very differently people feel, move and react to such an activity and, by extension, you can learn to appreciate these differences and accept them – both within the session and beyond it. Further, when you come to practise massage, familiarity with the energy patterns and interactive qualities of others will help to make your work more effective and appropriate to their needs. Finally, as Akong Rinpoche said, this exercise can help you to overcome fears of what others may be doing behind your back. As with all the other exercises, anyone who feels apprehensive about trying this should feel free to sit it out.

Back-to-back ★
Begin by standing (or sitting) back-to-back and simply feeling your partner through this contact. Reflect once again on your motivation, reaffirming your wish and intention to benefit your partner, to learn and to enjoy yourself. Make sure you keep breathing freely. When you feel ready, slowly begin to move. Try to keep a balance so that both of you are initiating movement and responding without one dominating the other. Take care that the movements you initiate do not cause pain or distress to your partner. If you keep your awareness open, you will be able to tell by an increase in tension if the other person cannot work with what you are doing.

See if you can communicate just by moving and sensing, without words or faces. You can lean and sway, twist and turn, rock and roll, gradually increasing the range of movement. There are no rules other than sensitivity and respect for the partner. By the same token if she/he is hurting you in some way, let them know. You are learning how to relax, not how to be a martyr. Some people automatically link arms when doing the exercises.

This may cause strain and limit the freedom of movement, but if both partners like it, it's okay.

SELF-HELP FOR THE BACK ♥

Since even the most languorous session of Back-to-Back may engage moving parts that haven't been used for a while, it may be a good idea at this stage to spare a few compassionate thoughts for the back itself. If the neck can suffer the stresses and strains of modern life, the area from the shoulders to the waist is vulnerable to an even wider range of complaints. If therefore you should experience serious stiffness or outright pain during any of the exercises that follow, it is important not to force anything. Either move on to the next exercise without the warning symbol or take a rest until tomorrow and see how it feels then.

Informed advice should always be sought for persistent back problems, but it is also true that many of the aches and pains associated with new or unfamiliar exercise are inherent in the training or developing process itself. So be aware of any bodily protest at, or resistance to, the practice and proceed patiently. Be as kind to yourself as you would be to others. Except in the case of a prior back injury or long-standing weakness, however, there is no reason why the following exercises should be harmful in any way.

Swinging from the waist and hanging off the wall ★
Stand upright with knees slightly bent and your feet a shoulders' width apart. Make sure you have space enough to swing your arms around. Let your arms hang like thick ropes from the shoulders. Keeping a stable upright axis, begin gently rhythmically to turn the upper body from one side to the other. As you twist from the waist to the left, let your loosely hanging arms follow. When you reach the limit of the twist to the left, swing back to the right, keeping a continuous side-to-side motion, with your loose arms following the swing on either side alternately.

Next, keeping a strong stance with knees slightly bent, hang forward from the waist. You can either allow the arms to hang

Swinging from the waist

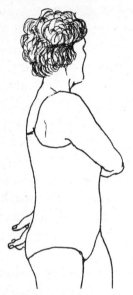

Hanging off the wall

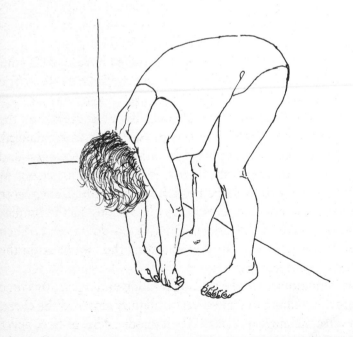

down loose or folded if it feels more comfortable. Vary the direction of swing from side to side to up and down, always using a minimum of effort and remaining as loose and floppy as possible. If this feels good to you, extend the swing from side to side with big swings like a pendulum, but always loose and relaxed.

When you feel you've had enough swinging, or if the swinging movement doesn't feel right, then just hang from the waist for a while. More relaxing still, back up to a wall and with your heels a few inches away, lean against it and just hang with arms folded or loose, either still or swaying gently. This is a lovely relaxation that can be done for a few minutes at almost any time or place. Practised regularly, it will little by little lengthen the hamstrings and help to release tension in the lower back. It can be especially helpful after sitting at a desk or computer for a few hours.

Knee-to-chest

The next two exercises, knee-to-chest and pelvic tilt, may sound like highly gymnastic disciplines but are, in fact, nothing of the sort. Indeed, those with lower-back problems will find them particularly beneficial, as they are among the gentlest of activities. They are also recommended if you wake up with a stiff back. As long as no sharp or sudden pain is felt, proceed as follows.

Lie down on your back on a mat or folded blanket with your neck gently extended and your chin tilted towards your chest. You may need a small pillow or rolled-up towel to keep this position without strain. Bring up the knees until both feet are flat on the floor and at a comfortable angle, with your body well-balanced. Now, very gradually, bring the right knee towards the chest and slowly fold it into your arms, thereby drawing it a little closer. At the same time try to keep the head, neck and shoulders as loose and relaxed as possible. Feel what's happening in the lumbar region, be aware of the stretching going on down there. Then reverse the process, ever so slowly, setting the foot back on the floor and feel the letting go.

Rest for a moment in the starting position and repeat, this time even slower, pulling the knee ever so slightly closer to the chest, and reverse the move as before. Try it another time or two, never straining but pulling the knee closer in towards the chest each time. Where there is stiffness it can help to 'breathe' into it, allowing the inflow to suffuse the area of tension. Allow the outflow to carry that tension or discomfort away.

Now try it several times with the left knee, always gently and carefully, returning to a restful position between each stretch. If you often wake with a stiff back it can be very helpful to do these knee-to-chest stretches before getting out of bed. This exercise can be a very relaxing way of easing yourself into the day.

The pelvic tilt

The pelvic tilt offers similar benefits, both in relaxing and strengthening the muscles in the abdomen and back. Lie down on a mat as before, knees bent, feet flat, but this time keep your arms outstretched, palms flat on the floor. Very slowly raise your tail bone forwards and upwards off the floor towards the ceiling, as high as feels comfortable without straining anything – and be aware of each vertebra as it lifts off, and then slowly touches down again, one by one, back to the starting position. Rest and relax for a good thirty seconds before repeating, as often as you like, but don't force or rush it.

The rocking chair ★

This exercise can be positively exhilarating, so needs to be approached with a little care. First, you need more than a mat on the floor. A folded blanket or thick carpet is advisable, as rocking around on an unyielding surface does the vertebrae no good at all. As you practise the exercise, therefore, take care not to stray off the padded surface on to a hard floor.

Sit with your legs loosely crossed and hold the left toes in your right hand, and the right toes in your left. Tuck your head forward and rock backwards as far as is comfortable. In fact, rock as far as the point of balance, from which it's perfectly natural to rock forwards again. So rock forwards head towards the floor, before gently throwing yourself back again. Repeat for as long as feels beneficial – or indeed exhilarating. Adventurous types with strong necks and shoulders can rock right over, indeed, turn upside down.

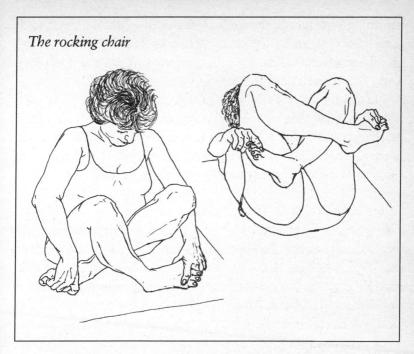

The rocking chair

But many people find rocking from tail bone to shoulders quite exciting enough.

Feel your circulation improving and the spinal nerves being stimulated as you rock back and forth in this most comforting of positions. This exercise is ideal for relaxing after a long period of inactivity and might also be described as self-massage of the back. As with all such activities, the body will tell you exactly what's good for you and what isn't. Don't try it after a heavy meal, for example! If your abdominal muscles are too weak to propel you effectively then, unless the weakness has some pathological basis, a few sit-ups done regularly will improve the situation over time.

Lying-down twist ★

Next we come to the lying-down twist, and yet again it carries the warning to stop if there is acute or sudden pain. In fact, this exercise is well-known for clearing stiffness and tension and can be most relaxing.

So lie on your back with the arms extended out from the shoul-

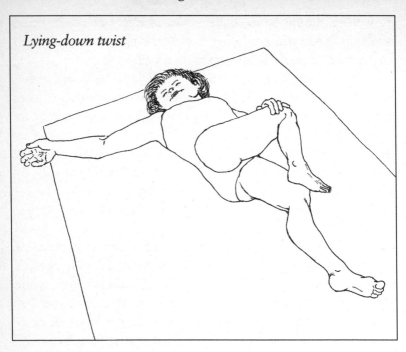

Lying-down twist

ders and the legs straight and together. First raise the right knee and rest the right foot on the left knee. Then, keeping the right arm fully extended, reach across with the left arm and slowly try to bring the right knee down towards the floor on your left, twisting your spine to help.

Try to keep the right shoulder in contact with the floor, with neck and both shoulders relaxed, and don't just grab or pull at the knee. Rather use the weight of the left arm gently to coax the knee down towards the floor. Feel how this subjects the spine to a thorough twist along its entire length – and if it feels stiff and unyielding at any point, breathe into that place. As you feel the inflow suffusing the problem area you might find you can let go a little more.

After two or three minutes relaxing into that position, return to the starting point – legs and arms outstretched – and feel the stability, the absence of twist in the spine. Repeat with the left foot on the right knee, right arm drawing the left knee down towards the floor. And again use the breath; work with it inside your body, gently letting go more and more. Whether alone or in a group situation there should be no sense either of effort or competition involved. What you are doing is discovering more freedom of movement and energy in your spine, that's all.

When working in a group it can be helpful to work with a partner in this exercise. While Partner A draws their right knee towards the floor with the left arm, Partner B can apply gentle but firm pressure to the right shoulder, holding it to the mat. This increases the effectiveness of the stretch. Partner B may also be able to help A to release a little more by bringing warmth by rubbing with the palm the area of greatest strain in the sacral area. But B must be careful not to push or force the stretch; this should remain completely under A's control.

Even on your own you may be able to increase the effectiveness of the stretch by hooking your right shoulder under a heavy piece of furniture such as a low bed, chest of drawers or sofa while gently coaxing the left knee towards the floor. Try to keep your left leg as straight as possible, but not too tense. Like most of the exercises in this guide, the true benefits of this stretch will only be discovered through many repetitions.

Off the wall stretch ★

The off the wall stretch is not quite as crazy as it sounds, but very effective for applying gentle traction to the spine. It should be done with care and gentleness and should you encounter sharp pain at any point, then leave this stretch alone. Likewise, if you know that, through an operation or for other reasons, any of the vertebrae which normally move freely are fused, it is best to leave this exercise alone unless you have advice of a trained Osteopath, Chiropractor, Orthopedic physician or other back specialist.

First lie down on the carpet or on the floor with a blanket, your bottom up against a clear space of wall about 1.5 m (5 ft) wide. Allow your legs to fall open in a V-shape just as far as happens naturally without pushing. If this stretch for the inner thighs is painful at first, the exercise can be done with the legs straight up the wall. However, the wide stretch is also effective for gradually stretching and releasing tight muscles in the inner thighs and helping to loosen the pelvis.

Off the wall stretch

Place the hands against the top of the thighs, as close as possible to the body. Then gradually straighten your arms until you can feel the stretch in your spine. Relax your body as much as possible and breathe deeply in and out very slowly five or six times. Then when you breathe out press a bit more. If you keep your lower back very relaxed, you should feel a stretch all the way up the spine, but especially at the base of the spine which is often very tight. If you are prepared to work with this stretch regularly and gradually over several months, you will find greater flexibility in the sacral area but also in the legs. You may find it easier to sit cross-legged.

The frog
This is a simple, yet invaluable exercise which, with a little practice, may become as much a part of your daily movement repertoire as sitting on a chair. However, if you are not already aware of your special areas of tightness, you may meet them here. Therefore, in the beginning it will help you to use cushions to adapt it to your weaknesses.

The frog

First kneel down on a folded blanket, carpet or mat. If there is discomfort at the ankles owing to contracted muscles protesting at being stretched in this way, provide them with the support of a rolled-up towel or something similar. Now, still kneeling, spread the knees as far apart as they will comfortably go, while keeping your toes together behind you. Pause, sitting back on the heels. Make sure your body is balanced and straight. This is a very strong sitting position. If it feels relaxing, you might rest your palms on the thighs and simply sit for a while.

Then bring the arms up and stretch them out above your head. Reach for the ceiling, before gradually bending forward from the waist. Keeping your bottom in contact with your heels, imagine that your belly is going to lie flat the floor. It won't, of course, but the image may help you to get the right stretch. As you imagine your belly touching the floor, extend your arms and hands as far forward along the floor as you can.

Hold the stretch for a moment or two, then relax, bringing the arms back and folding them under your forehead as a pillow. Rest like this, lying forward, loose and relaxed. If there is a lot of tension, put cushions under your chest, but continue the stretch. Feel the stretching at the base of the spine as its habitual compression is eased for the duration of the exercise. Once again, breathe into any areas of pain, gradually relaxing more and more.

The frog can be of great benefit to those whose jobs involve standing or sitting a lot, which can cause an ache or soreness across the sacral region of the spine. So, upon returning home from work, take a rest in this position before getting involved in something else. There may be some initial protest from the inner thighs, as well as the ankles, but a little gentle stretching won't ruin them; and they'll soon feel the benefits of increased flexibility and general fitness, particularly if you are able to practise regularly. If it is comfortable, you can even read in this position.

The benefits of this exercise can be further enhanced by giving a little self-massage at the same time. Try reaching behind and using a palm to address any area of stiffness. Clearly if you can't reach that far you can't, so perhaps a friend could help. Another suggestion, when in this position, is to lay a hot water bottle or heating pad upon any trouble-spot. At any rate, spend as much time as you can afford with the weight off your back and always remember to keep it warm. In my twenty years of practising massage and teaching relaxation, I have seen many individuals with chronic lower-back problems learn to manage their painful condition using the frog as a main remedy. It can also be a very comforting resting pose.

The shoulder stand ★
The shoulder stand can be most beneficial for the upper back and shoulders. An exercise borrowed from the Hatha Yoga tradition, it is advisable to ask an experienced practitioner for guidance before trying fully to extend your legs into the air. Personally, however, I find a modified version just as helpful in relieving upper-back strain.

In the modified version, while lying on your back, raise your knees towards your face. Then, gradually straighten your legs behind your head while supporting your back with both hands as it lifts off the mat to an angle of about 45 degrees. Draw your elbows as close together on the mat as you can. By changing the position of your legs – straightening, flexing, raising, extending, you can vary the intensity and placement of pressure on the shoulders and upper back. In this way you can release much tension in the shoulders and upper back. As with the rocking chair, it is important that this be done on a well-padded surface (at least two thicknesses of blanket) which is wide enough to accommodate both elbows. Your movements must be very slow and controlled to avoid accidental wrenching of muscles. So if you are not very fit, take it slowly. Try to breathe freely and evenly at all times. if you find this exercise beneficial, I recommend that you seek the help of a teacher, or experienced practitioner, of Hatha Yoga for instruction in the full shoulder stand.

Two simple relaxation techniques

Here are two ways of relieving stress and tension in the upper body which can be tried anytime and more or less anywhere. You may have been hunched over a screen or machine all day, or have a few minutes to spare before a meeting or a class. You might feel tired, stiff, bored, stressed-out or world weary. At any rate, spend those few minutes simply folding your arms in front of you and making circles with them – forwards, backwards, right and left, just as in the hand warm-ups (pages 36–41).

The other suggestion is to back up to a heavy piece of furniture or door-frame – so long as it's a stable, squared-off surface – and lean, press or rub those inaccessible parts against it. Not as good as a massage, obviously, but relaxing for tense, stiff shoulders nonetheless.

EXCHANGING AN UPPER-BODY MASSAGE ★

The massage that follows engages the hands, arms, shoulders and back, and there need be nothing formal about it. It's the kind of exchange that might commonly be offered to friends, colleagues or family members at work, at home, indeed wherever the need arises. As long as there is a chair or stool and someone to practise on, no further arrangements are necessary.

It's quite easy to tell if someone is suffering due to tension or stress of some kind. A hunched or rigid posture is often a clue to tension in the neck or shoulders which will readily respond to a gentle, caring massage. In fact, once you know how easy it is to help relieve some of that tension, it can actually be quite uncomfortable to be in the same room with someone who's enduring such suffering when the situation does not allow you the freedom to offer your help. As your compassion and fellow-feeling for others develops it becomes easier to identify both the nature of the problem and the best way of relieving it. Then it's just a short step to making the offer to help in a way that is neither threatening, patronising, embarrassing nor socially unacceptable. Over the years I've found that very few people are offended by the offer of a shoulder massage – if that offer is sensitively made – as the following anecdote suggests.

Some years ago, in Washington DC, I was teaching an evening relaxation class. I was explaining to a group how you should be ready to apply massage wherever such help is needed. One student was a martial arts exponent who would turn up to sessions in his Karate outfit. He was a big, burly man whom I found as intimidating as a nearly grown St Bernard puppy. He arrived early for the following session and told me he'd really learned a lot last time. He specifically mentioned being impressed by the notion of being prepared to give massage in any situation, according to one's motivation to help others.

It seemed that earlier that week he'd wandered into a downtown bar where a drunk was trying to pick a fight with anyone and everyone in the place. So our martial artist came over and told the man that what he needed, rather than a brawl, was to learn to relax a little. Then, right there in this rough and tough bar, he gave the man a shoulder rub which pricked the balloon of his aggression and had him in tears. Within a few minutes the man was calm.

Though I would never have encouraged such a bold approach, anything is possible when the right motivation is combined with confidence. As you become more sure of yourself and your ability to help others with your hands, you will be surprised how often conventional distance can dissolve as though it had never existed.

There are lots of situations, particularly with older people, those who have been ill or are depressed and frustrated with their situation, where such an attitude can lead to the best of all massages – unplanned, informal, simply doing what needs to be done.

All that said and done, there are still many situations where one's help, however well-intended, is not really wanted. We must also learn to be sensitive to these times and never impose our enthusiasm on those who feel better left to their own devices. We must also learn to make it easy for the other person to refuse our offer – never making someone feel they should accept our attention if they don't really want it.

Beginning the massage: the arms

The person receiving the massage sits down on a stool or sideways on a straight chair while you warm up your hands using whichever exercise you find most suitable.

First stand to your seated partner's right side. Raise the right arm by taking the hand in your left hand. Then gently support their right arm by holding it loosely beneath the elbow with your own right hand, so their forearm rests along the inside of yours. Now, with your left hand more or less encircling the shoulder, encourage your partner to let go and allow you to do the work while you gently rotate the shoulder joint by moving the arm at the elbow.

With previous experience of the Limp game (pages 72–73) it should be possible to tell if your partner is able to relax during this initial encounter. If not, using your own discretion, you may suggest they try to do so. Squeeze the shoulder with your whole palm. Then move down and give the rest of the upper arm similar attention. Use only light pressure, allowing your touch to convey warmth and communicate the harmlessness of your motivation. And let there be an exchange of feeling if possible, rather than just one-way traffic. Get a sense of the other's strength as well as their vulnerability, so that you are more precisely able to provide what help is needed. When a measure of familiarity and confidence have been established, move on to the next stage.

Deepening the massage

Place your left hand on your partner's right shoulder and take the right hand in your own, as though to shake it. Gently swing the arm from the wrist, stretch and loosen it a little. As the arm begins to feel freer, steer it through the moves and positions that come naturally and easily, without trying to force anything. Let your experience be your guide. What has felt good for you in the past probably feels good to others; similarly what hasn't, probably doesn't. Notice any restriction of movement or signs of discomfort which may be related to a medical condition – perhaps even in another part of the body. Where there is resistance or stiffness, perhaps there is also pain, so take it easy. If you have any doubts that what you are doing is actually benefiting the person – ask them.

Then, supporting the right arm with your right hand cupping the elbow, massage the upper arm with your left hand. A circular,

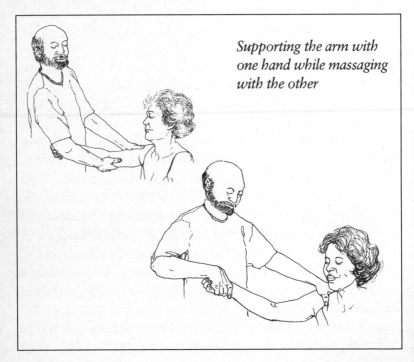

Supporting the arm with one hand while massaging with the other

kneading action is good, lightly gripping the upper arm between thumb and forefinger. You might also try some broader sweeps with the palm and heel of your hand. For greater sensitivity of feel, however, use your fingertips to gently trace the musculature and explore the intricacies of the elbow. Experience of your own body will tell you where sensitive spots such as the 'funny bone' are. By remaining lightly aware of your own sensations you may learn to 'map' or 'record' the work you have already done on the person you are massaging and this will help you to know where to go next.

Continue down the forearm, using the palm and fingers, although in practice the strokes should encourage the circulation in an upward direction, returning the blood to the heart. So while your progress along the arm is from the shoulder down, the flow of energy is balanced by massaging from the extremities towards the heart.

Move on to the wrist, employing thumb and fingers, and finally massage the hand, as in the previous hand massage (see pages 45–48), although not in such a detailed way. Afterwards, gently return the arm to its owner.

Improving the massage

During a relatively extensive massage like this there is considerable benefit in touching the various bodily bases with equal emphasis and attention, allowing the partner to feel the relatedness of these different parts. We often tend to experience the physical Universe in terms of a succession of incidents and transactions occurring here and there, now and then, in disjointed isolation. One moment there's a phone-call to make, employing the hand, ear and mouth; the next moment we have to process a meal via the throat and stomach. Thus some bodily functions are frequently, if not excessively engaged, while others may easily atrophy for want of exercise. A good general massage can correct such imbalance, restoring a degree of connection to the various points of contact with the outside world.

So if your hands discover a weakness or area of discomfort during their travels, it is important not to dwell on this place unduly. Whether the time available is long or short, equal attention should be paid to the whole arm, left and right, upper and lower, even to each individual finger. In this way the help given will be more readily integrated by the receiver, the massage will benefit his or her whole being more completely.

Now move on to the left arm and repeat the exercise. This will entail your moving round to a comfortable angle somewhere between the partner's left knee and shoulder. Follow the same routine as before, at the same speed and with the same degree of firmness.

The shoulders and spine
Once both arms have been helped to relax, move round behind your partner and cup the balls of both shoulders in your hands, fingers lying along the shoulders, making the connection between the parts you've just worked on and the parts to be massaged next. Then bring your hands along the shoulders in a long, slow stroke towards the base of the neck. Don't stop there but rather use the flat of the hands to continue on down the spine to the tailbone. Repeat several times, making a comprehensive connection between the arms and the base of the spine.

Before attending to the back in more detail you'll need to find a comfortable position that provides balance, stability and accessibility. Some may find it more convenient to kneel on a cushion. If you are right-handed, place yourself to the left of the sitter, and if you're left-handed position yourself to the right. This will enable you to get at the whole back with your main hand.

The back
Begin directly at the base of the skull and use the index and middle fingers, placed either side of the vertebrae, to trace your way down the spine, with just a gentle, up and down, rubbing action. Pay attention to the hollows between each pair of vertebrae and apply a little gentle pressure into these places. With delicate people – the elderly, very young, or those in poor health – the strokes can be positively feathery. Other bodies, heavy with fat or muscle, may provide only occasional clues as to the existence of vertebrae at all.

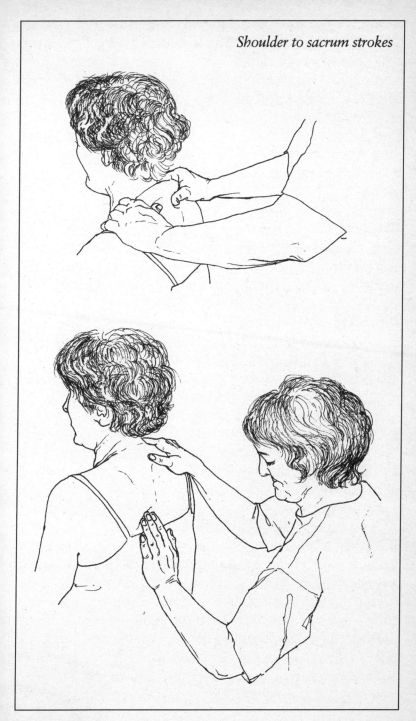

Shoulder to sacrum strokes

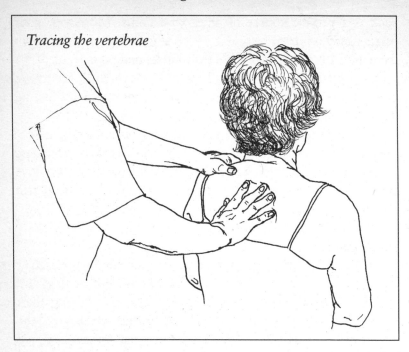

Tracing the vertebrae

In either case, as long as you have patience and the right motivation, the work will certainly have a beneficial effect.

Gradually and methodically, travel down the bumps and hollows to where the vertebrae widen at the junction with the pelvic bone – the sacrum. Move round behind the sitter and rest your hands on their hips, locating with your thumbs the slightly-raised points of the five, fused sacral vertebrae. Make gentle circles with your thumbs right along the pelvic bone from the sacrum to the hips. A lot of tension accumulates in these areas, so follow the thumb-massage with firmer, broader circles using the palm of your main hand. It is very good to imbue this contact with as much warmth as you can, as this area is often badly affected by cold.

It shouldn't be too difficult to generate compassion for the poor native of colder climes, obliged to move through life in a variety of essentially unnatural positions, enduring the stress, noise and pollution of modern life, not to mention the weather. Is it any wonder that the peoples of sunnier, more sedate regions find it easier to smile? In common with the neck and shoulders, then, the lower back is a prolific source of aches and pains. Moreover, your partner may not even be aware of the tension being stored down there until a little massage eases the muscles and takes some of the pressure off them. Take care, therefore, not to rush. Rest your hand on the sacrum, warm and supportive for a while, allowing the tension to unwind in its own time.

Now if your partner is in bad health, weak or frequently tired, it can be helpful gently to retrace the stages of this massage back up towards the base of the skull again. Most people, however, have more than enough upward-moving energy already, and so will benefit most from being worked on in a downward direction.

Finishing off

Conclude with work on the shoulders. Stand behind your partner with a hand resting on each shoulder and use both palms and thumbs to knead the top shoulder muscles, right along their lengths. Find the points between the spine and the curve of the shoulder blades and press and rub into them, one by one, applying as much controlled pressure as is comfortable. These points extend all the way from the place where the neck begins down to the lower tip of the shoulder blades.

Where you find muscles that are tense or knotted, ease off a little. Make circles with the thumbs or flat, stiff fingers, working into these places, patiently untangling the knots as though teasing the snarls out of wind-blown hair. Again, use only moderate pressure, according to your awareness of how the massage is being received. With patience and sensitivity on your part the tissue will gradually loosen, but do continue to pay attention to your partner's responses. Try not to drift away in some sort of repetitive daze.

If your partner wants to talk, it may help with the relaxation. Be careful not to fill the space of silence with your own topics as this kind of chat is likely to distract you and annoy your partner. However, like everything else, there are exceptions. Sometimes you will find yourself massaging someone who is extremely uneasy in the situation and their silence is an expression of unbearable anxiety. In such a moment, any light topic that comes to mind is likely to be more helpful than a more distressed silence. It is in such moments that it is especially important to remember to keep your breathing free and open along with your feeling for the other. Empathy will be your guide as to the best way to help your partner to feel at ease.

To finish off the massage you may like to make some long, sweeping strokes along the shoulders and down the arms, then along the shoulders and down the spine again. It's good to finish the massage as smoothly and respectfully as you began it, leaving the partner as gently as you can.

Receiving a back massage

When it is your turn to be the receiver, enjoy the experience and relax into it. Remember to keep breathing fully and use this opportunity to feel how the various moves your partner makes are being received by your own body. You might learn strokes you hadn't thought of but which feel good, while making a mental note of those which don't work so well. It is true to say that learning to relax is an on-going process. Your openness to someone who you have not even met yet who may one day need your help, or, who may be able to help you, means the learning process has no end.

Session Five

Think for a few moments. Can you say that you are completely satisfied with your life? No complaints? No second thoughts about family members or relationships? Dissatisfaction is almost a definition of what it means to be human. Many of us know we would like to be happy just as we are, but it's not so easy, is it? However, just as the white light visualisation can relieve physical suffering, the red light visualisation which follows is designed to address and alleviate the emotional turmoil arising from dissatisfaction.

Now there are as many causes leading to disagreeable emotional states as there are sources of comfort and joy in the world. Indeed, the whole cycle of birth, old age, sickness and death holds the seeds of suffering for all of us. But it is the way in which we react to life's changes that determines our state of mind at any given time. So what's the problem? Why are we so often unable to relax and accept things as they really are?

First, though we know intellectually that this life is impermanent, we behave as though we ought to live for ever. Anything that goes wrong becomes a very solid and important problem. With such a solid experience of ourselves, which we also project onto other people, animals and our environment, we create conditions for collision and conflict. Further, we are inclined to view the world and its events in terms of how they affect us personally. Thus some of the things that happen are seen as good and lucky for us – or positive – while others, the ones we'd prefer to be changed, are regarded as bad, unfortunate or negative. The trouble is, we don't always get what we want, or perhaps we get what we don't want. In either case, reality can conflict with our hopes, dreams or expectations, leading to disappointment.

The seeds of a great deal of dissatisfaction are sown in childhood. Family situations and environmental factors can have a considerable effect, while other conditions are hereditary. For example we are short when we'd rather be tall, or we are not as pretty or handsome as we'd like. We crave education, success, a family life; and when these achievements fail to make us happy we might wish we'd married someone else or never married at all. We want to be appreciated, remembered, loved; we want to amount to something in the world. This is understandable. What else seems real and valuable in a world of shifting certainties than to be loved and admired, to be as important to others as we are to ourselves?

However, if things don't go our way there can be emotional suffering that leads to resentment and anger: anger at those people and situations that annoy or demean us; envy, jealousy and pain. What begins as a vague dissatisfaction with our lives can easily become an attitude characterised by aggression, depression or some other negative reaction. On top of all that we may feel guilty for having these emotions and thus feel even worse.

One approach to dealing with these emotions is to suppress or deny them so we don't have face or deal with them. We may justify this approach, thinking we thereby limit their negative effects. Such an intention to protect others from our negativity is laudable enough – and if you can't help others at least you shouldn't harm them – but there is a saner way. Practising the red light visualisation can help us open up to the antidote to dissatisfaction, creating a feeling of fulfilment and satisfaction which precludes a sense of poverty and self-pity. Although the notion that our existence can be rich and precious occurs simply at the level of a visualisation at first, with growing confidence in the experience, an infinitely deeper satisfaction in our daily lives can be discovered. The experience of joy arising from within gives rise to recognition and appreciation of causes for happiness outside of us as well.

The red light also relates to the ability to express oneself. Many people feel frustrated and obstructed in their pursuit of happiness because they are unable either to communicate on equal terms with others – to be taken seriously perhaps – or to express themselves in creative activity. The red light helps clear such blockages, allowing self-expression to develop on a variety of levels.

The benefits of visualisation

It is said that one of the main differences between Asians and Westerners is that the former accept the inevitability of suffering in their lives and are grateful for every moment of happiness that comes their way, whereas the latter expect gratification and happiness as their due and are dissatisfied with anything less. It follows that if we can keep our disappointment under control, by regarding it as natural rather than cruel and unjust, or if we can transform it into smoke that disappears into the air, then a great number of emotional disorders and their associated physical symptoms may be relieved.

How these exercises are able to benefit others is rather less obvious, but with practice and the expanded awareness associated with such techniques, evidence is not so hard to find. Naturally, any positive improvement in our attitude will have a beneficial effect on those nearest and dearest, just as a warm smile can travel all around the world – as long as no one breaks the chain. But the visualisations could be effective on subtler levels too. The power of a kind or malicious thought about another being, however distant, should not be underestimated. How often do we think about someone and then they phone us? or find out later that they were thinking about us at the time when we were writing them a letter? More often our lives are so busy and distracting that we miss such signals, assuming instead that the coincidence was a random one. And yet if someone we loved were ill in some far country, wouldn't our impulse be to pray for them, or send out reassuring thoughts? If so, then these exercises may be useful, and they will certainly do no harm.

This is why the right motivation is so important. Generating a benevolent attitude towards those in need and sending out warm thoughts and loving kindness does everyone good. And gradually, with practice and experience, that goodness can increase and expand, to include more sentient beings within its warmth and light.

It is possible that practising the red light visualisation may give rise to, or stir up strong emotions, particularly where long-suppressed memories and feelings are concerned. This is quite natural and needn't be regarded as a threat. Just rest while the reaction passes and, without forcing anything, allow the light to do the healing work you designed and created it to do.

Thus the light is what you make it. It isn't a Buddhist, Moslem or Christian light – although it can be if you like. For though the restorative properties of light and love may be universal, the sphere that heals is your own creation, it stands for whatever you conceive as being pure and good. So it's more a matter of having confidence than holding any specific beliefs.

With confidence and patience, it is possible to work through a lifetime of problems and disorders in this natural and gentle way. Further, visualisation techniques can transform your perception of external events and others, so that they appear less solid, intrusive or threatening. You tend to become less self-conscious and more detached from unpleasant situations, so they have less potential to cause anger, pain and stress.

THE RED LIGHT VISUALISATION ♥

As with the white light visualisation, begin in a quiet, comfortable place and restful position and check your motivation. Give plenty of time to becoming aware of your body and the in-and-outflow of your breath, allowing your mind to settle. Of course, thoughts and impulses will continue to arise. That's fine – there is no need to suppress or censor them.

In this exercise you are going to work with this business of dissatisfaction, so allow yourself to review the various situations in your life that fall short of your ideals and expectations. Consider the hopes and dreams that haven't come true; any sorrow, regret, or anger you may feel about that. Remember any envy and jealousy associated with others having or getting what you wanted for yourself. These recollections may be deep-rooted or comparatively recent, intense or vague. The point is that you are aware of them, without reacting.

Then reflect on any wish you might have to express yourself to a particular person or via a creative medium – something you've intended to say or do, but which has so far been blocked or obstructed. Bearing these areas of dissatisfaction in mind, observe any associated physical sensations that may arise. Recall the feelings that occurred last time you felt frustrated in this way. Did you seethe, sweat, tense up, bristle, or cry perhaps? Was there pressure in the chest, a lump in the throat? Without forcing anything or acting out the emotion, simply notice it and settle back into the body and the breathing. Allow yourself to feel whatever comes up, but don't force anything. Keep your approach light and flexible, even as you touch into distressing memories. It may be painful to recall such experiences but don't worry. What you're doing is going to help you and, by extension, those around you to relax. Allow yourself to feel good about this – the aim is a noble one.

Working with the red light

Now, as in the white light exercise, imagine a completely open sky in front of you as seen from a high place. This can be a perfectly clear and cloudless, deep blue daytime sky, or a clear night sky filled with millions of stars. Relax your mind, simply gaze out with your inner eye upon this clear and open space.

From the centre of the space, a pin-point of light approaches, growing larger and brighter until it stops a comfortable distance away. Visualise it as a brilliant sphere, composed of five rainbow colours of light, expressing the five elements in their essential form. As the sphere revolves before you in space, remind yourself that these lights contain all the healing and restoring qualities of the whole Universe, the colours and elements constantly moving and changing, but always in balance and harmony.

Now the yellow of earth, the white of water, red of fire, green of air and blue of space dissolve, with all their powers and qualities, into a single rich red warm glowing light. This red light is very special and beautiful. It is not a heavy or violent red, but rather a light and joyous one; a loving red that inspires feelings of warmth and openness – like sunlight falling on a child's red balloon, or reflected in the heart of a flawless ruby.

The light approaches you and enters the body on an in-breath through a point at the base of the throat, spreading throughout the body, suffusing every cell with its comforting glow. Feel it trans-forming those pockets of dissatisfaction you have identified, soothing the pain and causing frustrations associated with blocked self-expression to melt away. Where there is the memory of not being loved, let there instead be a feeling of kindness and tender-ness that fills you completely. Where there is low self-esteem or lack of confidence, let the red light transform any sense of worth-lessness or vulnerability into a feeling of fulfilment and wholeness. And then, as your dissatisfaction is first diluted and then purified by contact with the red light, breathe out slowly and fully, expelling it as thick red-brown murky smoke.

This smoke carries away from the body all of your negativity, so that you are left filled only with the warm ruby light of joy and satisfaction. Little by little your out-breath becomes less smoky, your body sense less solid and your emotions more joyful. You are breathing out the same pure ruby light which you are breathing in.

If it works for you, think of others who are suffering emotion-ally or are blocked in their self-expression. Imagine the red light seeking them out, everywhere in the Universe, and purifying their suffering in a similar way. And rest in the feeling of fulfilment for a while.

Rounding off the visualisation

Finally, the red light flows back into the shining sphere, is re-absorbed into the redness, within which can now be seen the five rainbow lights once more, the five pure elements in constant harmony and flux, swirling and turning. Consider this pristine vision of healing light-energy and reflect that you can call up this appearance, bring it to mind whenever you want or need to, either for yourself or for the benefit of others.

Now the sphere moves away from you in space until it becomes a point of light in the far blue distance, then disappears. Allow the mind to rest completely. After a while have a good long stretch and sit up slowly. How was it for you? Perhaps the white light visualisation proved more effective, acting as it does on more phys-ical kinds of discomfort and pain. For others, the red light feels more appropriate. Of course, each colour contains the power of all five elements and can do the work of others, but since the different colours emphasise various levels and aspects of healing, it is useful to work with each of them from time to time.

SELF-MASSAGE OF THE HEAD AND NECK ♥

The next part of the session involves self-massage exercises for the shoulders, neck and head. They may be particularly useful for those whose occupation, or even leisure activities, lead to tension accumulating in these areas. Office work and other pursuits entailing sitting still for long periods, such as factory work, studying and watching too much TV, can all create stress, discomfort and stiffness in the upper regions of the body. Fortunately, as well as within formal sessions, these exercises can be practised whenever and wherever the need arises.

First warm up the hands as before (see pages 36–41), or if time is short simply shake them out. At any rate, finish the warm-up by rubbing the palms together until the hands are warm, loose and awake. As for the shoulders, the earlier exercises on pages 36–38 are recommended here. Finally, it can be relaxing to work along the top shoulder muscles with cupped hands, allowing the fingertips access to any tension there, not least in the shoulder joint itself.

The chest
Again the thumb and fingertips fit neatly into the points between the ribs, upper and lower, and relieve tension there. The points just below the collar bones are very helpful for relieving the kind of tension that comes from fatigue and anxiety. Press into them and breathe against the pressure. This may help to open the breathing in the upper chest.

Directly in the centre of the breast-bone is a point which is often sensitive, particularly among smokers and those trying to give up the noxious weed. Gently massaging this point can help to release toxins that have built up, and may also reduce the urge to smoke by reminding the body of the damage caused by smoking.

The neck

When self-massaging the neck there is always a functional problem since the very act of raising the arms to get at the neck creates muscular tension. However, adopting the frog position works well. Adopting this position as described on page 88–90, rest your forehead and elbows comfortably on a cushion so your hands are free to reach the neck without strain. Alternatively, if the frog is not really comfortable for you, try sitting at a desk or table and lean forward resting your forehead and elbows on a folded cloth or thin cushion.

Begin by squeezing the nape of the neck, as you might when petting a dog. Don't rush, but focus on doing all the movements in as relaxed and relaxing a way as possible. First squeeze with the right hand reinforced by the left on top, and then reverse the position of the hands. Next, move along the shoulders using flat fingers, alternately pressing and squeezing between fingers and thumbs.

Use whichever hand feels appropriate for each area while balancing the weight with the other. Give either side a good workout

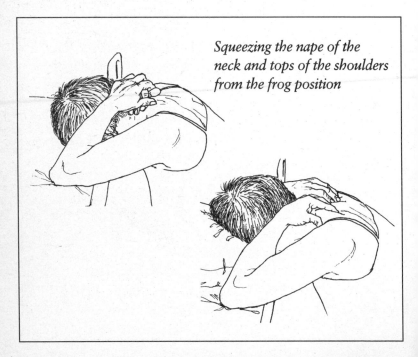

Squeezing the nape of the neck and tops of the shoulders from the frog position

before moving on to the vertebrae of the neck. With your finger-tips, press between the vertebrae. If you find sore spots, just hold them for a little while. Be gentle, though, as this area is commonly affected by a variety of structural and stress-related weaknesses. You can massage with light, circular pressure of the fingertips.

The base of the skull

This area requires rather firmer treatment, so depending on its sensitivity, use the thumbs as well as fingertips to circle up and under the place where the neck and skull conjoin. As well as tension, toxic residues, which are generally related to over-eating and drinking as well as worrying, tend to accumulate in this area. Attention to the base of the skull may well locate several points that will benefit from the exercise, clearing the neck and head considerably.

There is one pressure-point however, which should never be depressed continuously for more than a few seconds. This highly sensitive and effective spot is situated up and under the centre of the base of the skull and should always be treated carefully.

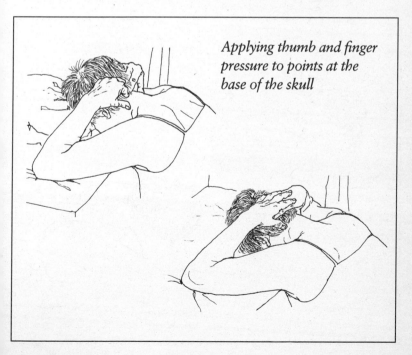

Applying thumb and finger pressure to points at the base of the skull

The throat

At the end of this stage return to an upright position very slowly, to avoid dizziness, before moving on to the throat. Here it's appropriate to make a distinction between the neck and the throat. For massage purposes, the neck consists of everything behind the ears and can stand comparatively stronger pressure than the throat, which is very sensitive and needs even more delicate handling. Both neck and throat, however, carry intricate networks supplying blood, air and nerve-impulses – as well as food and drink – and should always be massaged gently compared to more robust areas of the body, So in general use fingers rather than thumbs on the throat, and employ only light pressure.

Addressing certain points in the throat can have a calming, relaxing effect. Place the right hand on the left cheek – thumb pointing upwards, fingers spread across the ear and upper neck. Then, very slowly bring this hand down across the throat, just stroking lightly, down to the base of the throat a few times. Continue down to the chest if you like, as what you are doing is balancing the energy of the air element, which tends to rise disproportionately into the head. So coax it down, gently and slowly, to restore the balance. Repeat with the left hand on the right cheek.

Self-massage doesn't have to follow a precise formula or schedule; it is, by definition, a personal and individual affair. So evolve routines and strokes that feel right and proper for you, even rituals if you like, so long as the practice is truly relaxing.

Using the opposite hand, make a few small clockwise circles, from ear-lobe to clavicle, down the sides of the neck, fingers together and pressing in gently. Let the fingers stray into the hollow between throat and clavicle, as well as, once again, the hollow below the clavicle. A little gentle pressure here can have a releasing effect, improving circulation and clarity of thought.

Neck rolls ★

Apart from the various functions already mentioned, the neck and throat also have to support what is essentially a heavy spherical box of bone, containing brain, nerves for the whole body, fluids, sense organs, thoughts, impulses, emotions, cares and concerns. It also wears the mask we call a face and which many people feel holds their true identity. This can be a heavy load! In fact, by the age of 25 many of us are already losing mobility in the neck, so the first exercise carries something of a health-warning. Rolling the head around on the neck can be beneficial for all kinds of tension and is a good way to start the day but be sure you proceed very slowly and stop at any sharp point. Further, always take into account any medical history of neck or vertebrae problems. In such cases, professional guidance is advisable before proceeding. The exercise should always be carried out very slowly and gently, within the limits of ease and comfort dictated by the individual neck in question. Creaks, squeaks, crunching noises and protesting muscles can be expected at first, but acute pain is nature's way of telling you to stop.

Begin by allowing the head to fall slowly forward onto the chest. Now, very gently, begin to roll the neck to the right, taking account of any reluctance or resistance. Initially it can be a bit like getting the tangles out of long hair: if you comb too hard and fast the knots only get tighter, but with care and patience you can coax the tangles out. Stretch only as far as is comfortable, continuing

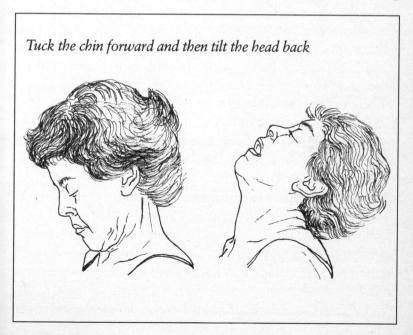

Tuck the chin forward and then tilt the head back

the roll round to the point where you are looking over your right shoulder. Then reverse the direction, continuing to circle until you are looking over your left shoulder.

It's important, whether sitting or standing, to keep the shoulders relaxed, and try to keep your breathing pattern regular and even. Starting in the same place, repeat the roll, this time first to the left, until the head feels thoroughly relaxed. As well as first thing in the morning, this exercise can be done anytime and anywhere to relieve stiffness, tension, and various kinds of headache.

Although the neck roll is a very complete workout for the neck, it is also helpful where there is chronic tension to exercise the neck with two specific movements. First tilt the head back as far as it will go. Then tilt the chin slowly forward and tuck it into your neck. Now press the back of the neck backwards while keeping your chin as far in as possible. Hold this pressed back position for ten seconds or so. Then tilt the head as far back as you can and hold again (see page 111).

Repeat this sequence 2–4 times, moving from one position to the other very slowly. You can do this several times a day to try to get rid of a stiff neck.

The head
There are, of course, as many varieties of headache as there are heads! And, like our thoughts and other mental phenomena, it is often difficult to figure out their cause, and therefore even harder to know the remedy. Certain categories of headache, however, and notably those related to eye-strain and either physical or mental tension, can generally be alleviated by the exercise that follows.

Start with a vigorous shampooing action, using thumbs and fingertips thoroughly to wake up the scalp and make contact with the skull. Then slow it right down because you need to locate specific points and apply gentle pressure with skilful fingers. This sequence should leave your head feeling clearer and better-balanced.

1. The first of these is situated right at the top of the head and is known as the anterior or frontal fontanelle. Seek out this slight

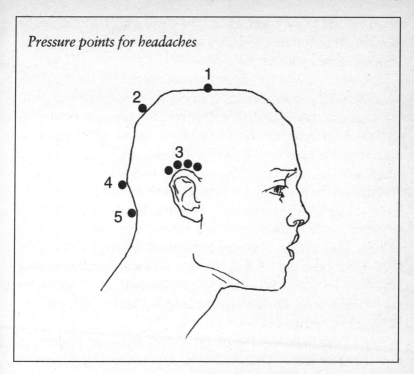

Pressure points for headaches

depression with the two index fingers and apply a few seconds' careful pressure.

2. The rear fontanelle is located at the back of the top of the head, where the hair grows in a circle. Use the index fingers, as with the anterior fontanelle, to press gently into this point for a few seconds.

3. Next there is a ridge above each ear, which may be sensitive whether or not there's an actual ache. At any rate it can be helpful, with all four fingers held together in a stiff claw, to press and circle a little into the shallow hollows beneath these ridges.

4. There is a hard bony ridge at the centre of the lower back of the skull. Press this very firmly.

5. Finally, just below, there's that most delicate spot, again up and

under the centre of the base of the skull. Press this with a lighter pressure and not for more than a few seconds.

The eyes

As well as being sensitive to light (which is often harsh in many public and working environments), dirty air, and a range of emotional reactions, the eyes are often obliged to work hard for long periods at repetitive or strain-inducing tasks. Such work may have to be done, but eye-strain and associated headaches can be alleviated or avoided by treating the eyes in a more kindly way.

Most physical work has its peaks and troughs of effort. For example, there is a rest-phase within each swing of the axe or shovel-full of earth. But where the eyes are concerned there is often a tendency to lock into the printed page, VDU or view of the road ahead, with only the act of blinking to compensate for the strain. It's a good idea, however, to slacken off such concentration two or three times every hour – not by switching to some other visual activity, but by relaxing the eyes rather more thoroughly. Of course, if you are driving along, it is advisable to pull off the road at this stage.

Now close your eyes, let the lids settle comfortably, and imagine the darkness as a wide open, far distant, empty space in front of you – or better still all around you – that has precisely the same air pressure, or any other kind of quality, as the space inside your head. There should be no resistance between inside and outside, indeed no distinction whatsoever.

With your eyes still closed, roll the eyeballs, letting them turn in their space as though they are simply floating there. Roll them three times to the right and three times to the left, in the biggest circles you comfortably can. Then open the eyes, still floating though, not trying to focus on anything, and apply the lightest of pressure to the following places: first, with the thumbs, into the inner corners of each eye; then, a little stronger, up under the ridge above the eyeballs, following the curve of the bony eye socket; and finally, with the index fingers and middle fingers together, work from the inner corners, along the lower sockets, towards the temples.

The temples seem to collect strain and stress-related tension, but you can clear a deal of excess air from the head by massaging them in a special way. Close your eyes again and place the fingers flat against the temples. Then with firm, but evenly-distributed pressure, describe backward moving circles – perhaps a dozen, long, slow turns. Afterwards, rub the hands together and rest their warm heels into the lower eye sockets, fingers spread across the forehead. Try to relax the eyes completely and rest like this for as long as feels natural – or at least for as much time as you can spare.

The whole exercise might only have taken a few minutes, but before re-opening the eyes and putting them back to work, try to recall exactly where you were before you took a break. Visualise if you can the very line or place where you left off, and when you return ease the eyes open at that place as gently as possible. Much of the benefit of resting the eyes can be lost if they are immediately set to frantic searching for a particular point in a text. Rather than snapping back to attention, to the reality of having this job to do, try to retain some of the spacious, relaxing quality of the exercise. A lot of headaches and eye-strain are caused by a kind of tunnel vision, so it's good to let go from time to time, whether within a relaxation session or whenever you can spare a few moments.

Another beneficial exercise that only takes a minute or two is near- and far-focusing. This technique can counter the negative effects of repetitive strain of the eyes such as a keyboard operator or precision manual worker might experience. First close your eyes and rest them for up to a minute, then look up, preferably into the far distance or at least as far as you can. Wait for the eyes to focus, then bring the focus back to your open palm, held in front of your face, as close as you can bring it. Focus on the lines of the palm for a moment, then up and outward again, far into space. Finally, rest for a minute or so with your eyes closed as loosely as you can, before returning smoothly to your work. This exercise can be repeated every 20 minutes or so during any protracted periods of work requiring close attention to detail.

Another kindness is to bathe the closed eyes with cool but not cold, water. It's also worth checking the quality or otherwise of the working environment itself. A great deal of eye-related strain and stress, for example, is caused by harsh or inadequate lighting; while certain heating and air-conditioning systems are unfriendly to eyes, not to mention throats and sinuses. These conditions can often be remedied, as can such factors as humidity, temperature and feng shui. If you work from your own office or room, of course it's easier to make the necessary adjustments; otherwise identify any deficiencies and point them out politely to the management – it's possible they hadn't even noticed.

The face

This self-massage session concludes with a little care and attention to the face – our most personal and powerful contact with what we generally refer to as the outside world. The various senses are clustered here, while processes such as ageing and the expression of emotions leave their imprint as surely as floodwaters erode the banks of a river.

First, the ears, delicate outposts of flesh, blood and cartilage are covered with acupuncture and pressure points. There is a branch

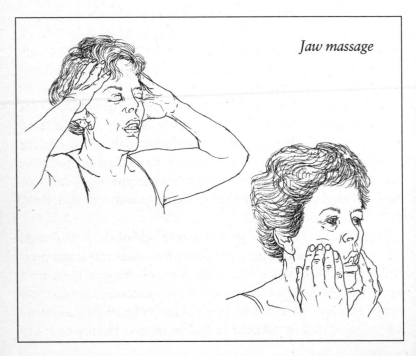

Jaw massage

of Chinese acupuncture that treats the whole body through the network of points in the ears. So thorough and skilful finger-work here can produce a variety of beneficial effects.

Starting with the lobes, use the thumb and fingertips to pinch gently all around both ears. Tugging on the lobes, folding the ears forward and allowing them to flap back, applying circular pressure to the upper ears, front and back, as well as rooting around in the ear-holes themselves, all of these techniques help to stimulate circulation and ease blockages in the system. In fact, giving the lobes a good pinch at sleepy or dull moments can stimulate points related to the head and awaken the consciousness in a simple and effective way.

Next, it's good to apply circular or rubbing pressure with the fingertips all along the gums of the upper and lower jaw. And since a lot of tooth and mouth disease is gum-related, massaging the roots of the teeth in this way can help to maintain the good circulation necessary for healthy gums.

Now pinch the lower jaw-bone between one thumb-tip and the knuckle of the forefingers, starting at the chin and working outwards. Use the fingers to press into the jaw-muscle where it hinges. Then open the mouth and describe downward and outward circles with the chin. Close the mouth again and repeat the exercise. Any pain or discomfort that occurs may well be symptomatic of recurrent frustration or repressed anger manifesting as a tender or swollen quality. It has been said that this area is the repository for all the anger felt towards those others in one's life, whom deep down we'd love to bite. At any rate, attention to the muscles of the jaw can alleviate such tension, loosening those clenched teeth. So practise opening and closing the mouth while pressing gently into the jaw-muscles, keeping the breathing deep and even and, don't try to force anything.

Then place the index fingers on either side of the nostrils and press against and along the cheekbones with moderate finger pressure. As you move along these bones, towards the ears, there are a number of sensitive points related to the accretion of tension and toxins. Similarly, at the boniest point of the bridge of the nose, there is a point related to congestion and stuffiness. Twenty or thirty

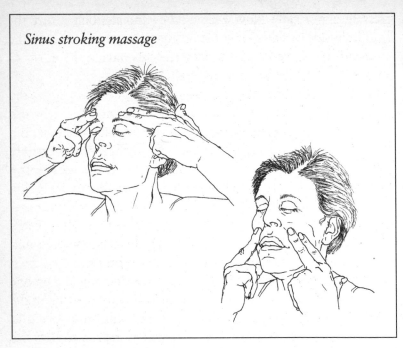

Sinus stroking massage

seconds after applying firm pressure on either side of the bridge of the nose, the sinuses will benefit and the nose clear itself. The sinuses also often respond to a gentle trailing of the index and middle fingers down from the inner corners of the eyes, down below the curve of the cheeks and past the corners of the mouth. Stroking outwards from the centre of the forehead towards the temples, again with two fingers, acts upon blockage of the upper sinuses.

One image to bear in mind during these sinus stroking exercises is of the fingers drawing clear, pure water down through the pathways and cleansing then. As well as having the right motivation, it can really help to inform such exercises with visualisations of this kind. By wishing strongly and also vividly imagining the practices that achieve their aim, their effectiveness can be greatly increased. It also diminishes the mind's tendency to wander off during the session.

For some people, the forehead is a battlefield of conflicting emotions, where a great deal of tension is both registered and stored. Try resting the heel of one hand on the ridge between the eyebrows and spreading the palm and fingers across the forehead, pressing quite firmly. Now, keeping the hand stationary, turn the head from side to side so that the palm and fingers drag across the forehead. It can be helpful to imagine this having the effect of pressing the wrinkles out of a silk scarf.

Of course, there are as many exercises designed to improve the complexion as there are anti-ageing lotions on the cosmetics market. The general rule, however, is to massage the face in a lateral or upward direction, although any technique that merely acts on the surface is unlikely to address the root causes of any underlying dissatisfaction and help either the skin or the being inside to relax. Indeed, agonising over wrinkles or one's appearance as a whole is hardly very relaxing at all. And yet how often do we find ourselves spruced up, made up, dressed to impress and making every effort to appear interesting to others, when we'd rather be curled up in a favourite old sweater looking like no one in particular at all? So the final exercise is called 'messing up the mask' and can help alleviate the stress and tension involved in taking oneself too seriously – particularly in regard to how we appear to others.

Close your eyes and imagine that your face is like rubber, a mask in fact, superficial to the real you. So rearrange it a little. Pull and push the mask into different faces that might be considered comic or grotesque – except that it really doesn't matter. Mess up your nose and ears, mouth and eyes, employing facial muscles and expressions that you don't ordinarily use. Now try it in front of a mirror and discover how varied your appearance can be. What we regard as our 'looks', or the image we prefer to project, is only one possibility among many. Don't try this with someone else's mask though, unless they specifically ask for such irreverent treatment – many people are not too keen on having their mask messed up.

EXCHANGING A BACK MASSAGE

Giving and receiving back massage, when undertaken with skill and consideration, can turn strangers into friends and promote deep, beneficial relaxation. The guiding principle is that if something would feel good to you, it probably will feel that way to your partner, but there are certain ground-rules that can make this more likely. So before you begin, you might like to consider the following points. First, the room should be pleasantly warm. Light, soft, loose-fitting clothes – with belts and watches removed – are advisable for both giver and receiver, unless you and your partner decide to work without clothing. We'll consider this option later, but, for the moment, here are some general suggestions.

Along with warmth and, ideally, peace and quiet, you will need a suitable working surface. The floor is fine, and often obligatory, but it should be padded and insulated against discomfort and cold. Folded blankets are good, or better still one of those thin camping mattresses that roll up. The important thing is that the surface doesn't subside when pressure is applied, so soft beds or mattresses are not recommended. And, of course, whatever you use shouldn't slip or slide around the floor.

Many people prefer to use a massage table or some other raised surface which is stable under pressure. Physical access aside, this is clearly a matter of individual choice. There are advantages and disadvantages to both floor and table, but if you do use the latter it should be level with the wrists when the arms are by your sides. Then the whole of the receiver's body is accessible without the giver having to stoop if the table is too low, or approach from an angle without sufficient leverage, should it be too high. It can be more tiring to work on the floor as this entails the giver getting up and down to move round the partner's body. On the other hand, such activity can constitute a beneficial workout in itself so, as always, practice is the best guide.

First, the partner should lie face down and get comfortable. It often helps to tuck a thin pillow or folded blanket under the chest, and another beneath the ankles. The first reduces strain on the neck, while the second prevents discomfort during work on the legs.

If you are using a table it's easy to move around the partner's back, whereas the floor option involves working on your knees. But in either case many receivers find it more comforting with the giver working alongside them rather than next to their heads, and this is worth considering. Certainly, it's not advisable to sit on the partner's bottom during a back massage, however convenient this might seem. The point is to allow the receiver to relax into the experience in as free and spacious a way as possible.

Work out the strokes you wish to try before the session and allow plenty of space for the exchange of back massage – don't rush anything. Where and when to have a session is once again up to you, but place and time should have that calm, spacious quality. If you are exchanging out of group time, you might spend 30 minutes or 2 hours each at first, and later find that an hour is ideal. Within the group session you will need to limit the back massage to about 30 minutes if both partners are going to have a turn. This may well mean leaving out some of the suggested strokes. If there is enough time once you have finished, you may want to leave your partner to relax while you take a break and make a pot of tea for both of you to enjoy. If possible, plan ahead and agree on how you will share the time, taking care that neither of you is rushed.

Good posture

If you are right-handed, stand, kneel or sit on a low stool or cushion to the left of the partner so that your right hand is level with the lower back and your left more or less level with the neck. If you are left-handed, start on the other side.

It is important to monitor your own posture and breathing as you work. Whether standing or sitting make sure you're not straining at any time, and that your breathing is neither constricted nor suppressed. The quality of the massage will very much depend on the physical and mental ease of the giver. Thus a tense, uncomfortable, distracted or bored practitioner will communicate these elements to the receiver. In this context it can help to visualise that your own energy is centred in the lower part of your body, that all movement originates in the abdomen, below the navel, and that the energy travels up and out through your hands, rather than down from the head and neck and out through your hands. This notion generally reduces effort and fatigue, as well as communicating a stable, centred quality of energy to the receiver.

Whether you are standing or sitting, try to feel evenly and stably balanced on your feet, knees, bottom and in yourself, so that the energy wells up from your centre in a constant and regular flow. Many disciplines concerned with both physical and spiritual healing and regeneration stress the importance of this central abdominal point and regard it as the source of our most vital energy. Most opera singers would agree. At any rate it never helps to feel that your energy is fizzing around haphazardly, or sparking out of your upper extremities. Find your central, lower balance, then, and work from the solid base and source of energy it provides. As you move around your partner, try to maintain the sense of balance.

Using oil

You might consider at this point the option of removing clothing to massage the back. Unless the room is really warm enough to prevent a chill for the person who is lying still, then forget it. But if temperature is no problem and neither partner feels shy about it, then there are advantages to massaging directly on the skin. If there is genuine trust, most people find skin to skin contact uniquely relaxing and nurturing. Though unless you have a little oil, you will be able to give a smoother massage through light clothing. So if you want to try massaging without clothing you must have an oil ready prepared.

The base for the oil should be light and neutral. Almond oil is probably the best, but any fresh nut or vegetable oil that doesn't offend your sense of smell is fine. Various massage systems stress the value of adding essential oils, of which there are countless varieties around the world. Many of these act upon and through the skin, as well as possessing aromatic qualities and the general rule would appear to be if you like it and find it beneficial, share it. Your roles as giver and receiver will be quite different, but sharing enjoyment of a scented oil helps to quickly bring you into a mutual space. Certainly uncorking the right blend can create an instant and positive bond between partners, leading to such ice-breaking banter as, 'ooh, that's a nice smell', and so on. So spend some time among the testing bottles at your nearest health food or natural cosmetics shop and design your own light scent.

It is worth researching specific benefits and contra-indications for any essential oil you might wish to use. However, if you use just a few drops of essential oil – just enough to scent the base oil – almost any of the essential oils that you prefer should be okay. The giving and receiving of massage is, by definition, a highly individual and personal experience. Choosing and blending your own oils can make it more so. If this aspect of massage appeals to you, there are any number of books on aromatherapy which could help you learn more.

Try it on yourself first. Find the right strength and quantity of oil to use and explore the differences between working through clothing and working with oils. Certain moves are more difficult through clothing because your hands cannot move as smoothly. Others, notably work on pressure points, are easier. It should quickly become obvious that using too much oil is always counterproductive, leading to excessive slipping and sliding, not to mention making a mess of the working surface, if not the wallpaper. Such hazards can be avoided by applying small amounts of oil to your own hands first, rather than splashing it directly onto the partner. One final piece of advice, based on a regrettable incident involving a Tabriz prayer mat, is to keep your oil in a bottle which has a lid that snaps easily and firmly shut between applications.

Making the initial contact

Bear in mind, however centred and balanced you may be, that some people feel uneasy about things going on behind their backs, so a calming and reassuring approach is always best. When you are ready, simply place your 'main' hand, fingers spread, lightly, but confidently, on the base of the spine, and your other hand upon the junction between the neck and shoulders. Rest there, gathering your awareness and best intentions for a moment, then place a hand on each shoulder blade and repeat. Finally, place your hands on top of each shoulder and slide them – palms open, slowly, but firmly, down the back to the base of the spine and rest there for a few moments. Repeat the stroke at least five times.

Another effective introductory stroke starts with your right hand on the partner's right shoulder and slides, gently but firmly, down the back to the sacrum. Meanwhile your left hand starts on

the left shoulder and repeats the move, so establishing a continuous, rhythmic flow of strokes down the partner's back. This can be
very relaxing for both of you. Centre yourself within the simplicity
of the exercise and feel it drawing any unease or tension down and
away. You may also discover where tension remains and know
better how to proceed next. Those starting out on the way of
massage might find this particularly helpful in establishing friendly
contact and reassurance.

A third way of checking whether your attentions are having
the desired relaxing effect involves a gentle rocking of the upper
body. Spread the fingers of both hands along the near-side of
your partner's spinal column, as a pianist might address a keyboard, and find for each finger the corresponding groove between
each vertebra. So if you are standing or sitting on the left side,
press the fingers into the grooves along that same side, causing
the upper body to rock away from you ever so slightly. Establish
a rhythmic rocking motion this way. Repeat this with your
fingers gradually moving down until you've covered the entire

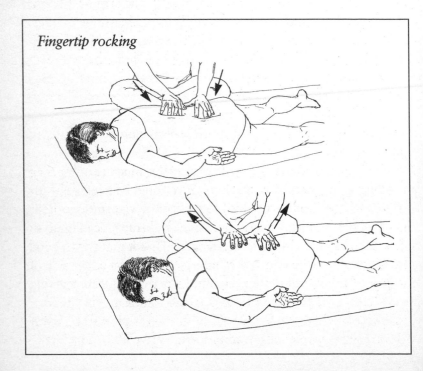

Fingertip rocking

length of the spine, from shoulders to bottom, rocking slowly and gently but continuously.

Now reach across the back to the corresponding grooves on the far side of the spine and press your fingertips into these, only this time gently pull the back towards you to establish a reverse rocking motion to complement the first. Again, repeat until all the vertebrae below the neck have been addressed.

This exercise should impose no strain on the back, so if there is resistance or stiffness in the partner's response, it probably indicates a lack of relaxation. In this case, working again from the left side, spread your left palm across the upper back between the shoulder blades and your right, firmly and squarely, across the sacrum. Now slowly push and pull the two areas being covered, setting up a rocking action between the independent and gently opposing movements of the upper and lower back.

This should help to ease any stiffness, and also help the partner become conscious that there's a whole lot of holding going on. Unless you are quite experienced and also know your partner well, it is probably best not to draw attention to the stiff as a board quality you've found in your partner's back. Many people feel deeply ashamed and threatened when they are unable to relax. They might feel you are picking on them or finding them inadequate in receiving massage. Silly as it sounds it is a common feeling and the last one you wish to engender in the name of relaxation. In general I try to wait until the person mentions it. Many times, though, the letting go happens over a number of sessions with nothing needing to be said

Many people find that one arm and hand is much stronger than the other, so in exercises of this kind there could be a tendency for one side of both bodies involved to get a more vigorous workout than the other. Remember, giving massage is therapeutic in itself, so it has to be balanced as well as integrated. Thus it is always a good idea to distribute the effort as evenly as possible on either side of the body, for your mutual benefit, and where this means moving around, it is good to keep your movements natural and balanced.

You are likely to encounter a deal of excess air energy when working with people who lead modern, active lives. The busily analytical, intellectual nature of such life-styles often manifests as mental restlessness, with a corresponding deficiency of the heavier, more stable elements symbolised by earth and water. A predominance of downward strokes can help neutralise this imbalance, while upward strokes are indicated where there is tiredness, depression, or the after-effects of an illness. Just as a working knowledge of anatomy and physiology is useful in the work, so is some feeling for the balance of the elements.

A question that often arises during massage sessions is whether or not it's advisable to hold conversations. Well of course if the receiver has some medical condition or experiences sudden discomfort they should say so. And if the two of you are well-acquainted there's no harm in engaging in a little light repartee. As for giving instructions or feedback during the session this can also be helpful but in general, with practice, you should be able to identify any problem areas by feel alone and make allowances and corrections accordingly. Telling someone to relax or let go might be helpful very occasionally, but such suggestions can often better be communicated by touch alone. Indeed, the root cause of any holding back or shallow breathing may be due to a lack of trust and confidence, which can in most cases be provided better through the hands. In many cases there is much to be said for silence, since idle chat or animated discussion can, in fact, be counter-productive as far as true relaxation is concerned. The rule I try to follow is to let conversation be initiated by the receiver and only talk if it seems helpful and reassuring for the other.

The shoulders
Time to work on the shoulders, then, kneading and pressing along the top of the shoulders from neck to arm-joint, easing out any tension you find. Some muscles will be tense or stiff, others knotted, and relaxing them may take time. Never mind. Most people enjoy having their shoulders rubbed, so you are unlikely to bore your partner. Leaning over and applying pressure can be tiring, though, so try to work with gravity as well as muscle-power. If you are using a table you could stand at its head to get the weight of your body behind the palms and heels of your hands if alongside feels difficult.

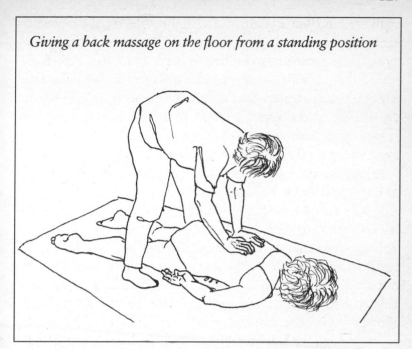

Giving a back massage on the floor from a standing position

Working on the floor allows other options. For example, you might stand astride your partner's back and use the heels of your hands and spread fingers, either crouching or bending from the waist. This is an especially useful approach when working on someone who has a large and well-muscled torso, because you can use the weight of your body without having to strain since you can distribute the workload more evenly across your own muscles and joints. Move around, finding the positions that feel most comfortable.

The shoulder blades

Tension often lurks here, and you can help your partner to release tension as follows: stand or kneel alongside to the left of your partner, with his or her face turned away from you. Bring their left arm, as long as it is not painful, up behind the back, in what is known in wrestling circles as the half-nelson position, while supporting the shoulder with your own left hand. Now with your right hand, thumb and forefinger extended, gently press the

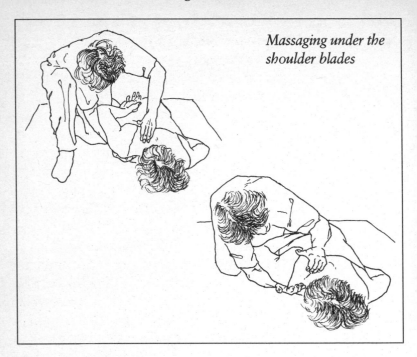

Massaging under the shoulder blades

exposed area beneath the shoulder blade. By very slightly jiggling the left arm with your own supporting one, you will open up this region even further. Be gentle, though. These are sensitive spots that harbour lots of upper-body tension, which should be released very carefully. Repeat from the right side, with your partner's head turned to the left.

Although this exercise can be really beneficial it is also one of the most difficult of the back massage positions to get right. There may be clumsiness or lack of co-ordination on your part, or your partner may resist being held in a half-nelson and jiggled about. Adapt your approach to the situation, the body in question, and if it still isn't working, phase it out and move on.

Moving down the spine
With both hands spread on either side of the spine, start at the shoulders and work down in small looping circles, applying suitable downward pressure, evenly and symmetrically, all the way down to the waist. Such terms as 'suitable', 'firm', 'gentle' and

'subtle' are merely guidelines – everything depends on the weight and strength of the receiver, their fitness or otherwise. Lighten the pressure as you approach the waist, as the area between the ribs and pelvis is unsupported when the body is in a prone position. Never apply firm pressure directly onto the spine itself, always press evenly to either side of the vertebrae.

Following a few of these descending loops, move on down along the sacroiliac joint. It is very important that both partners feel relaxed about touching in this area. Use your intuition and, if you feel uneasy, or pick up embarrassment from your partner, just leave it. Simply pressing along the ridge of the sacro-iliac joint on both sides, finishing with firm circular pressure into the hip joints, generally feels quite safe and beneficial. However, if both partners are relaxed about it, deep circular pressure into buttocks can be helpful for releasing tension in the lower back. Firm pressure with the thumbs on points that are sore to touch can sometimes relieve knee pain.

Across the back

Kneel or stand to one side and place your hands, fingers extended, on either side of the rib cage. Pull the far hand towards you and push the near hand away, maintaining sliding pressure against the back, back and forth, moving from under the armpits down to the waist a few times.

Then stretch out both arms and take a grip on the far flank, beneath the armpit. Pull with your palms and relaxed open fingers in a rolling, continuous motion, hand over hand along the one side, down to the waist. Repeat a few times then move round to the other side and repeat.

The penultimate exercise in a back massage involves a little light pummelling, and the key to successful pummelling is that your wrists and fingers should remain very limp. So rather than transmitting a series of shocks, try to bring a flexible, fluid quality to your work. Keeping both hands partly closed in very loose fists, arms and wrists relaxed, pummel with a continuous gentle action up and down the back – anywhere but directly on the vertebrae. Using the outer edge of the hands with fingers relaxed also feels

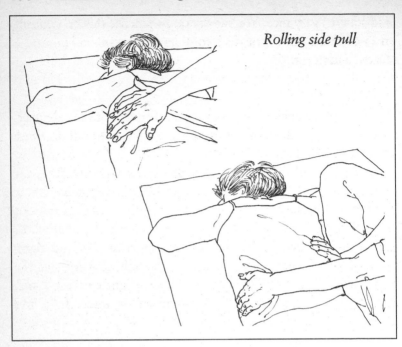

Rolling side pull

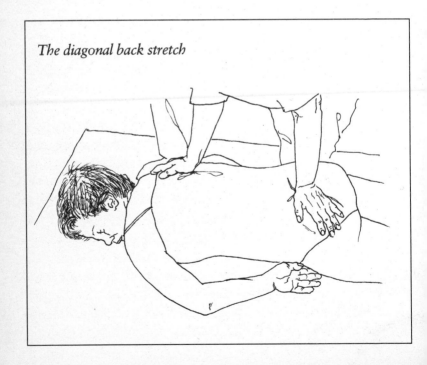

The diagonal back stretch

(and sounds) very nice. You may want to practise this on yourself, on your thigh, until you feel confident that your technique is relaxed and fluent.

Finishing off

Having kept in touch with your partner throughout the exchange, try to ease out of the massage as gently as you eased into it – with a final stretch and rest.

Kneel or stand to the right and place your right hand on the right shoulder and your left hand alongside the left pelvic bone. Now exert pressure, pushing in opposite directions, creating a diagonal stretch across the back. Hold this for a good twenty or thirty seconds before repeating from the opposite side. You might prompt your partner to breathe into the stretch, so increasing the benefit. Finish by simply laying your hands lightly on the spine, just as you began, before removing them slowly, respectfully, and letting go.

Session Six

During previous exercises we have worked with white and red light visualisations to purify physical and emotional disturbances respectively. Here, you will discover that by visualising the blue light, the problem areas of fear, anxiety, lack of confidence and, indeed, mental negativity in general are addressed in a positive way.

The way we see things and how we feel about them conditions our whole experience of life. If events, situations and other beings constantly fail to live up to our hopes and expectations we might start feeling unlucky, and a sense of disappointment and failure could set in. Similarly, if there is a lot of suffering or stress in our lives we might find ourselves looking out at the world from under a cloud. In either case, we are trapped in a cycle of perception, emotion and reaction that constantly disrupts our peace of mind. We are failing to see things as they are, to accept them for what they are, and to be relaxed about it. How then, can we hope to help others?

The blue light is designed to suffuse the consciousness with a spacious, inspiring, purifying blue light, transforming any dark pockets of mental negativity into smoke that dissolves harmlessly into the air in front of you.

THE BLUE LIGHT VISUALISATION ♥

As before, make yourself comfortable with as straight a back and neck as possible. Close your eyes and breathe peacefully, undisturbed, while your body and mind settle down to rest in a state of equanimity and balance. This isn't meant to sound easy but, since most thoughts and physical sensations are highly impermanent affairs, if you do not dwell on them they soon go away. So, for a few minutes, let things slow down a little.

Relax instead into the heaviness of your body, the simple rise and fall of your breath. Gradually, as the mind's superficial chatter slows and quietens, there's a chance for deeper, more personal thoughts and feelings to arise. Of course it's also possible you might sink into a lethargic daze but this, too, will pass. Reflect on any fear or anxiety you may detect at the back of your mind. Allow it to drift and swirl to the front and ask yourself what exactly you are worried about, what are you afraid of? This may be just a trivial sense of embarrassment at being seen with you shirt on backwards or it may be a deep, almost intrinsic fear, such as fear of madness or fear of death. It doesn't matter what comes to mind. The important thing is just to allow it to surface, with the confidence that it cannot overwhelm you, protected as you are by the blue light, the innate stability of the essence of your mind.

Don't try to get rid of or analyse your fears, simply bear witness to them. Allow yourself not to be so involved in these thoughts and feelings. Just as it's relaxing to watch the world go by from the window of a train without jumping out and trying to change something, so you can afford to watch your inner world for a while without getting tangled up in reactions to it. This won't necessarily be cosy: as already discussed, nothing is the hardest thing to do.

Allow at least 5 or 10 minutes to reflect on the events in your life that have resulted in fear, confusion, a sense of failure. Look also at your personal experience of mental disturbance, times when for whatever reason you could not think clearly or trust your own judgement. Often these situations, even in retrospect, still have the power to bring on a wave of anxiety. Without duplicating the traumatic feelings that caused that sore spot it can be helpful to recall some of the situations that made you what you are and still govern how you feel.

By looking more openly into your fears and the destructive reactions they have caused in your life, you can come to understand yourself better. You can see that many fears belong to the past. Any threat is long gone but the habit patterns remain, so you can learn to see through your anxiety and confusion – letting go of the past and daring to taste the present moment. The blue light can help to find the clarity and courage to do this often painful work for yourself and for the benefit of others. This is the right motivation, without which true development is unlikely to occur.

Introducing the blue light

Now, gaze with your inner eye into this deep blue, endless day or night-time sky. The sky is charged with all the colours and energy of light, in the centre of which appears a point of even brighter light, coming towards you. As it approaches, this light expands and fills to form a perfect sphere of swirling rainbow colours, the sphere of the five pure elements, which you now recognise from the previous exercises. You see the balancing golden-yellow light of the earth; the cohesive diamond white light of water; the warming ruby red light of fire; the intelligent emerald green light of the air; and the indescribably intense, deep blue light of space. All five of the lights now melt into the deepest of blue lights, the colour of lapis lazuli in the form of light. Just to look at this blue gives a feeling of courage and unshakeable confidence.

Now the blue light streams towards you from the sphere and enters your body at the level of the heart, in the centre of the chest. If this is difficult to visualise, imagine that the blue light enters your body with each in-breath, or showers into you unobstructed like rain through a net.

This light contains all the healing qualities of the Universe as expressed in the five colours condensed within it, and wherever it encounters fear and negativity it transforms and expels the emotions from the body as black-blue smoke which disappears into the air in front of you, leaving no trace. As the exercise progresses, the smoke is gradually purified, turning a lighter, cleaner colour. At the same time, be aware of any physical sensations related to the thoughts and feelings that arise. Breathe into those places and let the light thoroughly accomplish its soothing and cleansing work.

Presently, as the out-breaths grow clearer and the negativity you felt subsides, let go a little more and try to feel that your body is a little less solid than before, that it is suffused with the pure, spacious quality of the blue light. Indeed a physical sensation of lightness and relief may arise, that we have been able to let go of those deep anxieties which we had imagined to be so threatening, so real. Rest in this feeling of detachment, and allow yourself to experience a sense of confidence that you have found a way to free yourself from fear, confusion and helplessness.

Extending the visualisation

At this stage you might like to extend the practice to others who are locked into fearful or other extreme states of suffering. This can be either specifically to someone you know, or to all beings in general. In the first case bring that person to mind and imagine how it must be to have all of his or her suffering. In the second, think especially of all the children and animals in the world who are caught up in situations of war and violence, constantly uneasy and often terrified, bereaved or worse.

In either case, visualise that the stream or rain of healing blue light goes out to them from the sphere, enters their bodies and purifies all harmful and hurtful thoughts and feelings, leaving them peaceful and relaxed. There is no limit to the positiveness that is needed in the world, and no end to the potential for positiveness within us.

A personal experience

If this seems like a fanciful way of dealing with fear, I will give you an example of a time when the blue light visualisation may well have saved my life. I was living in Edinburgh and just recovering from a bout of bronchitis. It had been raining a lot but I had a few hours free and the sun was shining. It was a lovely day so a friend and I decided to take a walk up Arthur's Seat, a long craggy out-cropping that is one of Edinburgh's most distinctive landmarks. Its slopes were thick with purple heather and rusty bracken, as though covered with a tweed shawl.

Having been recently ill, I found the climb to the top utterly exhausting in spite of the fact that we'd taken one of the gentler, more winding paths. We were sitting out of the wind enjoying the sun and trying to find the tiny dot of my house down below, when the sky grew suddenly dark and a squall blew in from the Firth of Forth. We were dressed only in cotton and realised that we must find our way down as directly as possible. We could see a steep path straight down towards the house. Not one we'd ever taken, but it didn't seem wise to go back on the long windy one as it was now raining hard.

My friend, who was younger and fitter than I, led the way. It was steep and slippery, but all was well until a certain point where I found myself looking down through a curtain of rain onto a sheer stretch of slippery brown rock. My friend was below me and I could not imagine how she had got there as there was nowhere I could step. I was seized by a terror and was sure I would soon fall and die on the rocks below. It was so ridiculous! I was going to die on Arthur's Seat in the middle of the day within view of my own house. Then I remembered the blue light. I leaned back against the rock and closed my eyes invoking the very essence of courage and confidence into my heart. Along with it came the hidden stability of earth under my feet and the necessary fire to ward off the chilly wind. After a minute or two when I opened my eyes I could see the face of my friend and hear her words, 'You can do it. Just step a little down to the left there.' Sure enough, beyond the panic there was a place to step.

I was cold and shaky, but filled with gratitude to the blue light and to my friend as we made it down the hillside. By the time we reached home the sun was shining again. I tell this story just as an example of how very practical visualisation can be in helping us to face fear.

GROUP WORK

In those exercises involving backs we have worked with the fear of what's going on behind us and learned to trust our partner in this respect. The pushing hands exercise explores any apprehension we might have encountering others face to face, or indeed mask to mask. It is borrowed from the tai chi tradition, and is ideal for practising with several partners within a group session.

Some people might wonder how exercises like back-to-back (see page 80–81) and pushing hands (see below) belong in a relaxation course. However, a great deal of stress and suffering is caused by a sense of separateness between people, as opposed to a sense of empathy. Lack of understanding and care can lead to mistrust, animosity and fear. Since most disputes between people and peoples arise from a sense of otherness or territoriality, it follows that sharing a little space and playfulness can only reduce the likelihood of conflict in the world.

Akong Rinpoche has said that most human beings, particularly in the West, have considerable difficulty in co-ordinating themselves with others and in taking nourishment from contact with other human beings. He used the analogy of a child trying to learn to feed itself. The child picks up the spoon and brings it towards the mouth but the co-ordination is all wrong and the food goes everywhere. Frustrated but undeterred, the child tries again. This time the spoon misses the mouth and ends up all over the face. Closer, but not close enough. At this stage the combination of growing hunger and irritation turns into panic, you might even die before you get it right! Unless someone comes along in time to help the child in a compassionate and acceptable way the child may be too upset to eat even if fed. Similarly, when adult relationships with others have been difficult there is little confidence in the nourishment contact with others can bring, and it becomes impossible to co-ordinate emotional and territorial requirements.

So some of the exercises are designed to help the co-ordination of our feelings with those of others, and overcome the sense of separateness that underpins all tension and stress in the world. This is particularly true of giving and receiving massage, which can be a powerful expression of trust and sharing.

Pushing hands

The previous friendliness exercise had one partner driving while the other was a passenger but in pushing hands the steering job is shared. Simply stand facing a partner with your palms touching, and be prepared to lead or follow, advance or retreat, stretch or recoil, according only to the limitations imposed by maintaining hand to hand contact. Don't worry if your palms are not fully connected all the time. Even a finger's touch will do. Start very slowly and explore and be guided within the space defined by the length of your arms as freely and openly as possible. Close your eyes if it helps you relax but better still be aware of the person in front of you, with whom you are sharing and dancing in this space. You have your feelings about the situation and life in general and they have theirs, but for a few minutes you are both going to stop taking everything seriously and play a little.

Remain aware that there is another person's thoughts and feelings involved here too. Try to feel rather than think through what's happening. Keep the positive motivation – the wish that your partner should be well and happy – clear in your mind even as you express and enjoy yourself. If both partners focus in this way, a warm and sensitive exchange can naturally develop even when there was fear and self-consciousness at the start. If there is time in the session, complete the exercise with at least two partners so you may once more experience the uniqueness of each person's contact.

SELF-MASSAGE OF THE LEGS AND ABDOMEN ♥

The legs and abdomen are two parts of the body which can be massaged just as effectively by oneself as by others, not least because many people find these areas highly sensitive. Doing it yourself allows you to concentrate on finding out which strokes are most relaxing without having to experience any unpleasant surprises.

A great number of people, particularly those whose job involves working with others, manage successfully enough to present a smooth relaxed upper body and face to the world, but that doesn't always mean they are not under stress or experiencing tension. In fact, they may not even recognise or acknowledge that they are. Often the ability to remain calm and controlled on the surface can lead to tension being stored elsewhere – notably the lower back, legs and abdomen. Fortunately, it is possible to get at the latter two places, where a little regular self-massage can be most beneficial.

A great many leg problems, especially in later years, are related to the moving parts – the joints – and the circulation. As with the back, climate can be a factor here, so always dress warmly when exposed to the cold and damp. Another common cause of stiffness and discomfort is the more obvious one of having to work standing up – for example, in a shop, outdoors, or even as a massage therapist. One solution is to set aside some time regularly to lie down or take the weight off the feet and legs. Let them rest higher than the head, say on cushions or up against a wall. As for massaging these areas, any existing or potential problem related to the circulation of the blood in the legs should be taken into account before proceeding. And always be especially gentle with older people, whose skin and veins may be delicate and sensitive.

It's not advisable, remember, to apply any kind of pressure to varicose veins. There is one technique that can help, however, and this is best done last thing at night before going to bed. Using a flexible shower-hose, direct cold water onto the feet and legs, working in an upward direction. Then dry vigorously in the same direction, before spending a few minutes with the feet above the level of the head. The benefit can be felt immediately.

Apart from standing around a lot, another activity that can lead to discomfort in the legs is the otherwise relaxing practice of sitting cross-legged in some kind of meditation posture. Newcomers may find this a particular problem, but the following massage should help.

Leg warmer

Sit on the floor or mat with your legs straight out in front of you. Hold a kneecap lightly in each hand, and jiggle your legs from side to side. Now, working up from the feet to the knees, use the flat of your hands to briskly rub with the open palms, one palm on either side of the shin, rubbing with the same kind of heat-producing action and pressure as you use when rubbing your hands together to raise warmth. Massage the legs in an upwards direction in this way, as firmly as feels right.

When you get to the knees it can feel very good to rub all round them with warm, cupped palms, so easing any tension in the joints. To get at the calves you will need to cross one leg over the other, with the knee raised, and again use as much pressure as is comfortable to iron out any stiffness in these muscles. In fact, you might find you can breathe more easily after a little work on the calves.

The upper legs

Try crossing your hands beneath each thigh and pulling and pushing simultaneously in opposite directions. The tops of the thighs will also benefit from some kneading and firm circles made with the heel of the hand towards the groin on the inner thigh and the hip on the outer. Whether you use the heel of the hand, flat or cupped palm, or some kind of thumb and finger grip, the main thing is that these large muscles should get a thorough workout. This will help compensate for all the hours of the day they spend in fixed or tense positions. As for the hip, and outer thighs, try lying on your side on blankets or a mat – with a cushion for support – while rubbing and pressing into the raised hip.

Standing knee rotation

To help relieve sore knees, stand with legs bent, knees and feet together, and with both hands fully gripping and supporting both

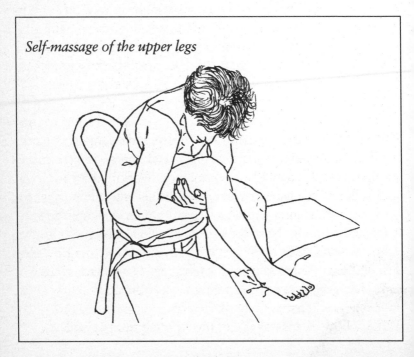

Self-massage of the upper legs

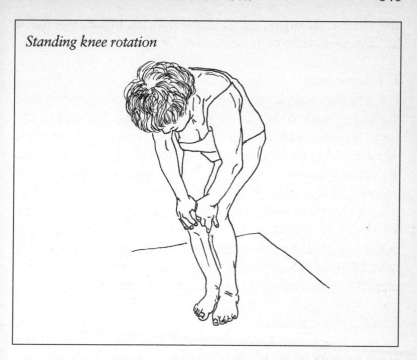

Standing knee rotation

knees. Describe as full a circle as possible in the movement of your knees, circling five times to the right and five times to the left. Alternatively, stand on one leg and kick out with the other a few times. Be careful not to snap too hard against the knee-joint, though, or to allow any twisting motion into the kick.

The abdomen ★

This is an area where special care is needed. Indeed, many doctors, particularly in Asia, insist that massaging the abdomen in the wrong way could actually be dangerous. Working on your own body will provide useful pointers but the general rule is never to work against the intestinal flow. This follows a clockwise course, so when massaging the abdomen you should always move up the right side starting at the pelvic bone, across below the rib cage, then on down the left side as far as the pelvic bone once again. To make the massage easier, lie on your back with your knees bent as this relaxes the muscles of the abdomen.

The following massages can be very helpful, particularly for

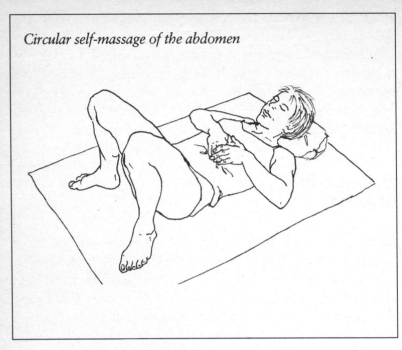

Circular self-massage of the abdomen

those suffering from constipation, whether caused by abdominal tension or otherwise. A little rubbing in the ways outlined below before getting up in the morning followed by a glass of hot water from a flask by the bed can ease this complaint considerably.

Just laying your warm hands on the abdomen can also bring great relief when the tummy is upset and growly. For women suffering period pains, just resting the warm hands still lower on the belly can alleviate menstrual discomfort. Apart from simply resting warm hands, however, note that these exercises are not advisable during pregnancy, or where there is unexplained heat or strong pain anywhere in the abdomen.

Keep the fingers of each hand flat and together. Place one hand over the other to reinforce it, then make small clockwise circles in a clockwise direction. Imagine your abdomen as a clockface with the navel at its centre. Massage around the outer edge of the abdominal cavity, beginning just inside the right pelvic bone and circling in small circles towards the navel. Continue slowly round and round the 'clockface'. Working with one hand on top of the other one can increase the pressure and depth as necessary with little strain.

Another useful stroke is to work from one side of the abdomen to the other using the heel of the hand, easing off at the navel before continuing across, and then using flat fingers to pull the flesh towards the navel before letting go. If you have a sensitive stomach put only the lightest pressure into these strokes.

EXCHANGING A NECK AND HEAD MASSAGE ★

As always, it is important to treat someone else's head with great care and respect. Indeed, some people are highly sensitive to having their heads touched at all and find it difficult to relax in such a situation. So, as with the abdominal exercises, it is a good idea to practise on yourself first. Knowing in advance which strokes are pleasant and relaxing and which are not will give you confidence in the work, confidence that will be communicated to the partner.

The neck and head massage can be done with the partner either seated on a chair, or lying down on his or her back. In either case, position yourself behind and above the head in question and let the first contact be merely to lay your hands on the other's shoulders. This indirect approach can help overcome apprehension and sensitivity while at the same time establishing the connectedness between the upper body and the head.

Beginning the head massage

The instructions here are for giving a head massage when the partner is lying down. This gives much more flexibility and opportunity for full relaxation and should be used whenever possible. However, it is important to know that you can adapt the instructions for use with a seated person because there are many situations where you can apply this massage when it's not practical for the person to lie down. Headaches happen often in the workplace where five minutes of head massage right at the desk might help.

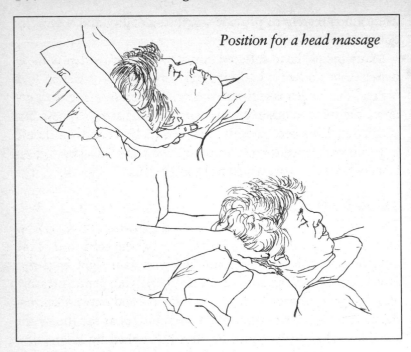

Position for a head massage

Physically, the head is sturdy as well as heavy. If you think of it as something like a melon, this may help you to know how to treat it. You can squeeze it quite hard, but don't drop it. The neck, however, as conduit for the nervous, circulatory and respiratory systems, requires great delicacy of touch. So always be careful not to drop the head suddenly or jerk it around. In fact, to persuade someone to release control of the neck muscles and thoroughly relax, you'll need to reassure that person that they are in safe hands.

Begin by cupping your hands to make a cradle for the head, supporting its weight in a comforting way. Be careful, though, not to apply inadvertent pressure with the thumbs to the throat. Nothing so quickly dispels a sense of safety as a justified fear of strangulation, even if it was accidental. Now, gently and ever so slowly, raise the head, bringing the chin towards the chest. Stop at the point of resistance and return to the starting position. Next allow the head to fall to the right, and then to the left. The weight of the head itself will supply all the energy needed for these turns.

Your job is merely to provide support, stability and a sense of direction.

Many people have suffered injury to the neck, often without consciously knowing it. Moreover, any degree of tilt or turn beyond that which is entirely comfortable can transmit pressure down the spine to other, possibly problematic areas. If these first encounters have been sensitive and skilful, however, you should feel your partner starting to trust you and relax. As always, your first guide will be what would feel good to you.

The neck and shoulders

The next exercise, if your partner is lying down, involves raising the head to get at the neck and shoulders. Lift the head clear of the table or mat with your left hand and with your right fingertips travel down from the base of the skull applying gentle pressure into the space between each pair of vertebrae and outwards across the neck muscles. Continue along the muscles at the top of the shoulder, where firmer pressure can be applied by means of a squeezing motion. Change hands as smoothly as you can and repeat the exercise down the neck and along the opposite shoulder, before gently returning the head to its starting position.

Now find a position where you can comfortably get your thumbs into the shoulder muscles, along both shoulders and down into the curve of the shoulder blades. This area often accumulates a great deal of tension, so use your thumbs and fingertips in tandem, working out along the top ridge of each shoulder to include the shoulder-joints themselves. Upon reaching the upper arms you can bring your palms into play and work quite firmly into these muscles, but always in a downward direction, out and away from the head and neck.

It is possible, of course, to massage the head in a variety of ways but my own rule is to work with the idea of directing the energy – and any stored tension – down and away through the arms, rather than in the opposite direction. In fact, certain individuals find that having their energy channelled upwards into the head can be positively distressing. I have heard of instances where such a massage has actually triggered an epileptic fit.

Working deeper into the shoulder blades

With your partner lying on his or her back, the opportunity may be taken to massage into the points between the spine and shoulder blades. This is an ideal position to get at these often tense and sometimes painful areas. Where stiffness and discomfort exist there may be resistance to letting anything in, particularly pressure from above. However, by sliding your palms underneath the upper back and seeking out the points with careful fingertips, you can reduce the likelihood of resistance. After all, since it's the weight of the receiver's body causing pressure rather than anyone else's efforts; he or she is always in control.

Start by introducing a hand, palm up, beneath the back to the level of the heart, with your fingertips in line, perhaps 2.5 cm (1 in) away from the spine, to one side or the other. Raise your fingertips, braced against the receiver's weight, according to his or her tolerance and your own physical strength, and allow from 10 to 60 seconds of pressure, again according to these conditions. Once you have managed to get your hand underneath in the right position, encourage your partner to let the upper body be limp and heavy, like a sack of potatoes.

For additional reassurance, or healing warmth – but only if it feels appropriate – you can place your free hand, palm spread, directly above the other, on the partner's chest. This will help you to balance and centre the upward pressure, as well as monitor the work in progress. Repeat with your hands a little further up towards the neck, alternately pressing and releasing, aware of the effect each move is creating. For just as each body differs in its suitability for firm or gentle treatment, so each part of that body will be relatively strong or weak. When you have thoroughly covered and felt along one side of the spine, change hands and repeat for the other side.

As well as alleviating stiffness and tension, this work can also help open the upper chest to deeper, more relaxing breathing patterns and habits. But, as with the head and neck massage, it's important not to stop when you reach the shoulders, leaving the energy still travelling upwards towards the head. Tidy any stress or tension you've released by coaxing it down along the shoulders and out through the arms.

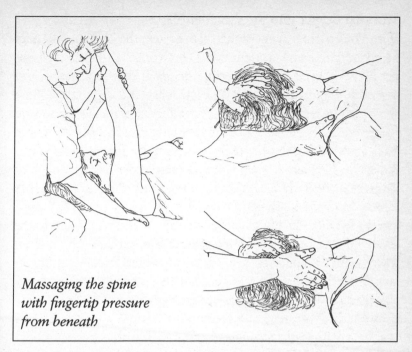

Massaging the spine
with fingertip pressure
from beneath

Returning to the shoulders and arms

Return to the shoulders and arms to give them a rather more comprehensive workout. Start with the head tilted forward and supported by your free hand, while you massage in clockwise circles down from the base of the skull, paying particular attention to any hard, stiff or lumpy areas. These can be patiently addressed by means of the thumbs, fingertips, or heels of the hands – the images are of gliding, smoothing, soothing away the tension.

With the head still tilted and supported, grasp the nape of the neck between your thumb and the edge of your forefinger and press gently a few times. Change hands and repeat before returning the head to a comfortable, resting position on a small firm cushion, book or your foot. Use the fingertips ever so gently to work into the base of the skull. Once again, small circles seem the most relaxing, and you can work gradually down, pressing gently in between each set of vertebrae until you reach the shoulders. Since this is a more muscular area, put the thumbs to work here. Too much pressure and the receiver will tense up or squirm – too little and you're likely to tickle at best. Use your senses and feelings at every stage, and be guided by them.

Try working quite firmly into the larger muscles along the top of the shoulders. The effects of many working habits, whether caused by strain itself or bad posture, can knot these muscles really tightly and it may require considerable effort, as well as skill and compassion, to relax them. So, if your partner resists a bit, or groans a little, don't stop work altogether and give up – just try to be aware of the difference between beneficial discomfort and the harmful kind, and between short and long-term pain.

Finishing off

Towards the end of a head massage, I've found that most people enjoy a little gentle traction. If for any reason, however, you know or suspect this may be contra-indicated, simply leave out this stage. Otherwise, form a cradle with your two hands, supporting the base of the skull and remembering to keep your thumbs clear of your partner's throat. Now lean away from your partner's head – thus extending the neck ever so slightly. This extension is best accomplished on the partner's out-breath, maintained during the in-breath and released on another out-breath. You might also hold the stretch for two complete cycles, perhaps even increasing it gently on the second out-breath. It is important to be sure that you are pulling in an absolutely straight line. Repeat four or five times, and then return the head to a resting position.

Finally, here are two other suggestions for finishing touches, designed to leave your partner relieved of any residual tension and thoroughly relaxed. First, place your hands with straight fingers and spread thumbs on either side of the head and apply steadily-increasing pressure to both sides at once. Let this pressure build, very gradually, for up to half a minute. Hold for 10 seconds or so, then just as gradually ease off the pressure and rest. Let your partner's subtle responses be your guide to the amount of pressure that can be sustained without creating tension. Always be prepared to err on the side of gentleness.

Second, cradle and support the head with one hand and spread your free palm across the forehead. Again very gently, apply squeezing pressure, before just as gently releasing and letting go.

These simple neck extensions and head presses, if done smoothly, carefully and with respect, are a good way of bringing the session to a close. If it feels right, you might also like to rest your hands on either side of the forehead for a few long moments.

Finish by kneeling or standing beside your partner, placing a hand upon each of the shoulders, and gliding down along the arms to the hands, with a feeling of drawing off the residual tension. Continue down the hips, down along the outside of the legs to the feet, and rest your hands there for a while, before smoothly letting go.

In these finishing strokes, the end of the full body massage is anticipated. Whatever part or parts of the body you are massaging, you will always do well to take care with the way you finish off. It is good to be aware of the condition of the whole body and enquire of your partner if there's anything that feels it specially needs doing. Even if there is not much time, you may be able to simply rest your hands on any area that feels disconnected and then bring the session to an end at the feet.

Session Seven

The last session is designed to be practised over a whole day for those who have been working together as a group or as partners. It would be good to plan a lunch break, bringing food to share, or going out to eat at some place convenient and congenial. Putting together all the pieces you have learned into a full-body massage forms the main practice for each of two sessions, exchanging roles after lunch. There will also be time for some relaxation and free work with colour. So come prepared with paints, crayons, or pens and paper. If you have been working your way through the sessions on your own, invite a friend to receive a massage and perhaps share some of the other activities with you. Otherwise, you can just make your way through the different exercises in your own time, practising all the stretching and self-massage exercises you have learned instead of the full body exchange.

The purpose of setting aside the better part of a day for this stage of *Healing Relaxation* is mainly to consolidate what you have already learned. Also if you have met six times as a group, each time deepening your commitment to developing a more compassionate way of being with yourself and others, it can be very rewarding to spend a bit more time together. You may want to talk together about the possibility of further meetings to continue the practice. A few suggestions on this will come at the end.

RELAXATION SESSION: BREATHING AND FEELING ♥

Before moving on to the full-body massage, pause briefly to reflect on the importance and value of the relaxation exercises you have already learned.

You have learned to relax by focusing on your breath. You have also learned to go inside your body with your awareness to experience feelings and sensations arising and passing away moment by moment. Little by little you are learning to relax within this experience even when unfamiliar or painful thoughts, feelings or sensations arise. As you go deeper into the experience of relaxation what you learn about yourself becomes the foundation for what you are able to pass on to others. You can't really expect to bring someone else to a deeper state of relaxation than you have experienced for yourself.

Begin with a review session of the breathing and feeling exercise from Session Two (page 56–60). Have one member of the group read it out loud or you may have a copy of the cassette tape of these exercises which is available from Tara Rokpa, and you could play the appropriate part of the tape. Try to establish as full an awareness as possible of how the breath travels within the body. Try not to be concerned about the cause or origin of this or that sensation, but rather allow your mind to remain open and free from analysis and interpretation, simply noting the sensations as they arise.

Whatever thoughts, feelings, images or changes occur in this or other exercises, try to accept them just as they come, and then let them go. You could easily allow 20 to 30 minutes for the exercise.

EXCHANGING A WHOLE-BODY MASSAGE

Next comes a session of whole-body massage. If you are working alone, your time is your own, but if you are able to exchange all you have learned with a partner, make sure you divide the available time equally. It will take at least an hour each to cover all the areas we've mentioned so far, and how long you allocate to each area within that period must also be balanced. Probably it is best to plan for one person to give the massage in the morning and the other after lunch.

Since the main idea is to draw from everything you've learned during previous sessions, feel free at any stage to look at the earlier exercises and to make your own plan for getting around the body.

As you become more experienced you will find you start differently with different people. However, I don't think you can ever go wrong by starting with the feet. The alternative is to start with the head, but many people feel a little nervous with a direct approach to the head. There's a bit of distance involved with the feet which can be quite reassuring at the opening stage of a full-body massage. You can also work both gently and firmly on the feet from the outset, according to what is needed, whereas the head demands a lighter, subtler touch which may be more readily accomplished once you have warmed up and your partner is already quite relaxed. In fact, a good foot massage relaxes the whole of the body, so as you move on to the other parts the work is already well under way. I'd go as far as to say that if you've only got time or energy enough to massage one part of the body, usually a foot massage is the most effective.

If your partner starts out in a noticeably tense or agitated condition you might want to work from the upper body downwards finishing with the feet. In that case, you still probably would not start with the head. A slow, thorough hand massage can be one of the most calming and reassuring approaches. Then you can work on arms, head, neck, upper torso and down the legs ending with the feet. You can see by now that flexibility is an important consideration in massage. There is no one formula or routine that works for everyone. As you work more and more, you are likely to hit on two or three basic patterns for a whole-body massage, but you will still want to be flexible in how this may be applied. Whichever approach you take, end up holding the feet for a minute or so half way through the massage, as described below.

Beginning the massage
Begin with your partner lying on his or her back. Make sure that the rest of the body has all the support it needs at the head, knees and ankles and that your partner is everywhere comfortable and warm; muscles stiffen and tense up when they're cold. So in colder climates you not only have to get used to giving massage through clothing, but you also have to keep covered the parts not directly involved.

Having relaxed yourself and warmed up your hands, take one foot in each and simply hold them for a few moments. You might imagine your warmth and compassion flowing into the partner, but the main thing is to make a smooth and reassuring initial contact. The other point is to start in a position that takes in both sides of the body. Since you will often be working on one side of the body at a time, it's good that the first gesture should be a balanced one. So wrap your hands around the toes, or hold the feet, palms to the soles, and just relax together for a short while. Proceed to give a thorough foot massage based on your previous practise experience (see pages 76–77). You can start with either foot.

If your partner should become ticklish, remember calm contact with the palm usually settles this. By moving next to the toes, you will be able to massage each toe thoroughly, a rather fiddly piece of work, before moving on to the main body of the foot. Then try whatever strokes, presses, methods you have already learned in working on your own and others' feet. If at any point you find yourself getting a little out of touch, you might find it helpful to visualise yourself receiving the massage rather than the other way around, and feel as precisely as possible what that might be like. This is not something you would want to do throughout a massage, but rather as a way of bringing what you are doing more deeply into focus. It may also remind you if you've missed anything. Encourage your partner to tell you if anything doesn't feel right.

You may have experienced or looked a little way into one of the systems which attribute connections to other parts of the body from points in the feet. However, it isn't necessary to know which points on the feet govern what exactly, as long as you vary the pressure according to local sensitivity and make a point of massaging the whole of both feet very thoroughly. Whenever you hit painful spots, ease off and proceed patiently using less pressure, or coming back to it before you finish the session.

The legs

Next lift one leg off the floor or table with one hand cupping the heel and the other under the knee. Very slowly bend the knee and

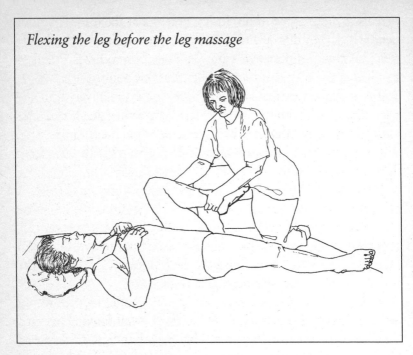

Flexing the leg before the leg massage

bring it up towards the chest – as far as it will go easily. Then swing it gently from side to side, before returning the leg to the extended position and repeating the move with the other leg. At all times bear in mind that your partner's legs are a part of your friend's body rather than hinged lumps of wood.

Before beginning to massage the lower leg, check to make sure your partner does not suffer from varicose veins. Should that be the case, just a gentle hold with the palms at various points up the leg on either side feels quite soothing.

Now move on to the shins and with moderate pressure from flattened palms and straight fingers try quite vigorous but smallish rubbing strokes up both sides of each shin from the ankle to the knee. Clearly the brisker the rub the warmer it gets. This is very good for circulation. Be sure to stop when you get to the knees, which is where some people start feeling shy and therefore uneasy.

The next move involves gripping a kneecap gently but firmly in each hand and aiming to roll both legs side to side from the hips. Your partner's body will tell you how he or she feels about this, perhaps by tensing up and refusing to let go at the hips. For some people it is very difficult to give up control of their legs. Should there be some resistance or emotional reaction to having the legs handled in this way, use your discretion at this point.

Knees can be very ticklish, so be sure to use a relatively firm and reassuring touch with the whole palm, along either side of the knee joint. This can be followed by squeezing of the muscles on either side just above the knee accompanied by sliding the thumbs from the centre out to either side.

By now you will be able to tell whether or not your partner is able to relax into the leg massage. Don't be discouraged if this does not seem to be the case. You can finish this part very nicely simply by placing your hand which is closest to the foot on top of the knee, and your other hand on the hip joint. This makes the connection in feeling with the upper body.

Move to the other leg and give it equal time, incorporating whatever you have learned of what works well for this partner. Don't forget that just stopping with your hands resting in one place and attending to your own breathing and motivation will always feel fine to your partner. This gives you the chance to collect yourself and feel what is the best way to proceed.

If your partner has appreciated the work you have done on the legs so far, you can proceed to massage the upper leg. This should consist mainly of long strokes with the palm up the outside of the leg and over the hip joint. You can also use big circles along the outside of the leg from the knee to the hip. This circling stroke with the palm can be especially beneficial if applied to the hip joint itself. Finish with the holding position of knee and hip mentioned above and then proceed to the other leg.

Working up the torso

Work your way up the body with a variation of the rolling side pull that you learned as part of the back massage in Session Five (page 129–131). You can do this from armpit to hip, first along one flank and then the other. It feels very good to most people and if you are not going to massage the abdomen should give a feeling of inclusion to the upper body from the face-up position.

The arms

Working down from the shoulder joint, use both hands to squeeze, stroke, push and pull all along the arm to the wrist, one arm at a time as described on page 93–95. Describe each stroke towards the shoulder rather than tugging the flesh towards the wrists. If you like, trace the muscles with your thumb and forefinger, seeking out the pressure points and circle into them a little. Keep coming back to the motivation that you really want all beings and parts of beings – this arm in particular – to be happy and relaxed. And don't neglect to move your own body as necessary so you can work without straining anything or restricting your breathing.

When you get to the hand it's good to sit comfortably beside your partner and rest the arm with the elbow on a cushion. In this position you can concentrate on the hand without having to support its weight as well. Use fingertips to make contact with sensitive points along the base of the fingers and thumb. Give the joints a gentle workout, stretching and pulling. But be careful not to overdo this bit by jerking the fingers or cracking the knuckles. Remember that most people experience their hands as being very close to how they feel themselves. If a person suffers from low self-esteem it is especially important to try to express your kindness and respect for who they really are. When you've finished one arm, lay it carefully down and move around to address the other.

Some people insist on maintaining hand-contact with the partner throughout a massage. While there may be occasions when it's reassuring to keep in touch at all times, such as when someone is feeling particularly insecure, in general this isn't really necessary. The important thing is that each time your hands leave the body they convey the message that they'll be right back. So don't jump from one part of the body to the other if you can help it.

The shoulders and chest

Begin this part of the massage by sitting or standing behind your partner's head for a minute or two simply resting both your hands just below the clavicle, with your fingertips meeting right at the centre of the chest. If your partner is a woman you may wish to reassure her that you will only be working on points right in the centre of the chest and above the breasts so she does not need to be anxious about what you might have in mind next. It would also give her the opportunity to say if she does not feel comfortable being touched in this area, in which case you can proceed to the shoulders.

Otherwise, with your hands simply resting and sensing, note the rise and fall of the upper chest as the breath flows in and out of the lungs. In many people, there will be almost no movement in this area to begin with. This could be because they are still nervous of the massage or that they habitually stop the breath short of reaching up into this area. If the breathing pattern changes and becomes shallower still, this probably signifies that he or she is wondering what you're going to do next. You could explain a little and suggest they just continue to breathe normally.

Meanwhile, locate the pressure points where the breast-bone and upper ribs meet. There are small notches all along this junction and a little gentle massage into these points can be most relaxing. Try to work in time with the breathing, particularly when applying pressure into the centre of the upper body at the level of the heart. As your partner breathes out, apply the pressure, and ease off as he or she breathes in again.

Continue like this for a while, particularly if the breathing is shallow, or noticeably suppressed. Using pressure skilfully on this part of the body can send a signal to open the upper breathing area. If the receiver gets this message during a session they may also remember later how relaxing it can be to breathe more fully and be able to correct their day-to-day breathing pattern accordingly, and so might you.

Rather than asking your partner to sit up as you move to the shoulders, create a space beneath the shoulders by lifting one arm by the hand with your free hand and sliding the other hand, palm upwards, into that space. When you release the raised arm you will be well placed to apply a series of upward presses from the base of the shoulders up to the neck, as you have already learned on pages 146–47. Remember, don't apply the pressure directly to the spine, though. Instead, start just to one side and move up gradually. Afterwards, move around, change hands and repeat for the other side.

The neck and head

Recall the strokes and presses involved in the neck and head massage as described on pages 143–46. Don't be concerned about missing anything out, simply make the moves that you do remember in as thorough and evenly-balanced way as possible.

Stabilising the body's energy

Bring the energy back down to earth again by using both hands to make long, steady strokes from the top of the head, down the side of the neck, shoulders, arms and upper body. Continue from the waist down the outside legs and finish off holding the feet, much as you began. If you find or feel that the upper body still has a congested or restricted quality, repeat these strokes from the head down, perhaps this time imagining warmth and relaxation radiating from your hands. Emphasise the wholeness, and of course the connectedness of the body during this phase, and communicate this emphasis through your touch. End up holding the feet for a minute or two before inviting your partner to roll over on to his or her front.

When in this position, it is often more comfortable to put a cushion under the chest, so that the head and neck are subjected to less strain and tension when, necessarily, they are turned to one side or the other. Although many massage tables are designed with face-holes or cradles for the head, a cushion under the chest is fine. The main thing is that the head and neck should feel equally relaxed whichever way they are facing.

The back

Once your partner is comfortable – perhaps after laying your hands on the back to re-establish contact – make some long strokes down the back from the shoulders to the hips. Use any strokes that have worked before (see pages 123–31) as well as new ones appropriate to the person. Ease off if there's any sharp or sudden pain. It is usually good to ask your partner if they have any injuries or special problems with the back. If so, be particularly careful not to work in a way that might cause pain. Obviously you are not qualified to treat a medical condition, but often patient, gentle massage, which communicates genuine warmth and care, will ease the suffering.

Sometimes it's obvious when you hit a sore spot but people who expect massage to hurt might be quite good at grinning and bearing pain, so be mindful of tell-tale tension appearing elsewhere in the body – gritted teeth perhaps. Point out that what you're doing shouldn't hurt and suggest they speak out if anything is painful.

It's good to use some of the larger moves that involve several muscle groups at once, to work generally as well as locally. Whenever you've been working on a particular area or on certain points, it feels good to balance this with longer more inclusive strokes.

Moving on from the back, a little work on the buttocks may be in order. At this point you could encounter resistance of some kind through, say, shyness or embarrassment. One approach is to point out that the lumbar and sacral regions can store enormous amounts of tension, indeed outright discomfort. Apply moderate pressure with the thumbs along either side of the coccyx and up along the sacrum, along the sacroiliac towards the hip joints. This load-bearing system comes in for some hard treatment during the average lifetime and the stresses and strains involved lead to all kinds of aches and pains. Be gentle with these often sensitive points and balance this precision-work with some firm pressure into the buttock muscles. The heels of the hands can work together, in outward moving circles side by side, down from the waist to the upper thighs, then up and across to the hips. Work well into the hip joints with whatever amount of pressure seems appropriate. However, if massage in this area makes your partner uncomfortable, move on.

The backs of the legs

Work along the outside of the thighs, using long sliding strokes from above the knee to the hip. Sensitivity in this region is often related to a touch that is too light or sharp, so describe a series of big, firmish circles with your flat palms. If you feel the partner is responding to the treatment, pulling handfuls of thigh muscles, hand over hand, from the inside to the outside down each leg can be even more relaxing.

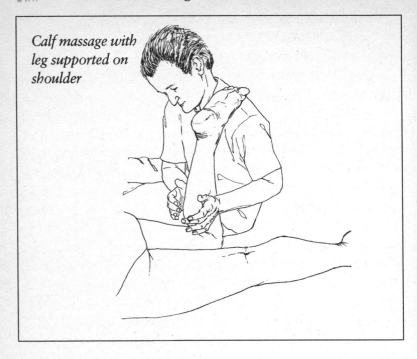

Calf massage with leg supported on shoulder

The knees are another notoriously ticklish area. It's usually possible, however, to use the heels of your hand to apply light pressure around the sides of the knees. Perhaps more effective is to work into the muscles above and below the hollows at the back. You can work very easily into the calf muscles by resting each ankle in turn over your shoulder. This leaves both hands free and allows the entire calf muscles to hang freely.

Start by gently pressing the heels of your hands into the belly of the muscle. From this contact you should be able to determine how sensitive this muscle is, and how much pressure to employ. Of course, you can also do this with the leg lying flat on the floor or table, but not so freely.

People who lead athletic lives, or who walk and stand a lot, store a deal of lactic acid in this area. This stroke can help a great deal, but be gentle. Afterwards, smoothly descend to the feet. Press them wherever and however seems appropriate. Finish by holding both feet firmly around the toes.

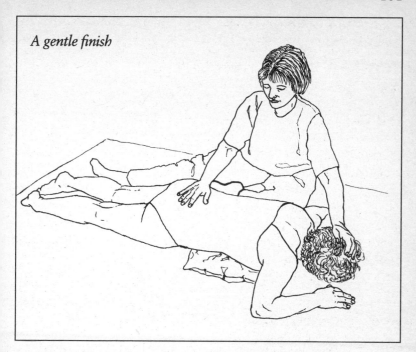

A gentle finish

Finishing off

Place your left hand upon the base of the spine, while hooking your right arm under the ankles. Now bring both lower legs up so that they bend at the knees and the heels approach the buttocks. They won't actually touch unless your partner is relatively supple, so just hold the legs at the point of resistance for 10–20 seconds. This exercise has both releasing and energising qualities.

Let the legs down gently and bring your awareness to bear on the whole body, from heel to toes. Stand, kneel or sit to the left of your partner and place your right hand on the sacrum, the very base of the spine, and let it rest there, warm and comforting.

Now place you left hand first on the top of the head for a moment, second on the back of the neck, and finally just rest it gently on the upper spine at the heart region. As you make these connections you may feel the same connections being made inside yourself; relax into the qualities of alignment and balance they represent. When it feels right, slowly remove your hands and suggest, in a quiet voice, that you have finished the massage, but there's no rush. You may then wish to go to make a cup of tea for each of you.

You can rest for a while, both of you. You have helped each other to relax and only good has come of it. Moreover you've both worked together in an open way for an hour or so – quite possibly emotionally as well as physically – and nothing bad happened. It will probably be that much easier to relax next time you work with a partner. Not that you need to wait that long before reaffirming the most important aspects – the motivation to help others and the wish to develop compassion.

DEVELOPING COMPASSION

Everyday life throws up numerous opportunities to share a little of our richness with others. Of course, we don't have to massage every aggressive drunk we meet. We'd be ill-advised to do so. But having a generally relaxed and compassionate attitude can help to generate peace and happiness in the world. Relaxing words can also be helpful, rather than feeling we have to win every argument. And the remarkable thing is that whatever you have given hasn't been lost or wasted, let alone exhausted. The more you give, the more you find you have to give.

Sometimes you might come across a person with whom it's difficult to make contact. He or she might be tense inside or otherwise beyond your reach. In this case you might have to try a little harder – not physically or mentally but spiritually. Instead of becoming bored or frustrated with the lack of effectiveness of the work, pause to renew your motivation and generate a little compassion.

It can be nice to massage a beautiful fragrant body or someone you care about and then hardly any compassion is required. But when the partner is not so blessed or loveable, or is unresponsive to your efforts, it is harder to remain open and warm. You might not be quite so naturally motivated to give help in the first place, and more easily tempted to give up on that person. Or you might grow bored, lost in daydreams and go through the motions in a mechanical way. In any case there won't be much benefit for either you or the person you are working on.

One way to counter such tendencies is to remind yourself how fortunate you are and how rich is the situation. You are strong enough to lay aside your own concerns for a while and consciously develop your humanity in a basic and unselfish way. With good intentions and a few simple techniques you can aspire to generate warmth where none existed and to help someone else feel better. Consider, too, that right here on the floor this potential friend might be prepared to submit to your attentions because he or she admits to needing help. See if you can get some sense of the suffering that lies behind their resistance to massage. Try to find the thread of care and respect without forcing anything.

Often in such a case it is wise to keep the massage short and simple. It is also good to be able to sense, and admit to yourself, when you are out of your depth. Carefully explain that you lack experience and feel that it is best to just do a short session for the time being. A cup of tea can often cover the remaining distance.

Alternatively, you might just take a few deep breaths and get on with it. Since helping someone to relax is in itself a compassionate act, it could be argued that all you have to do is simply be there in as warm, open and aware a way as you are able, and you will probably do some good. If you don't necessarily expect anything amazing to happen, you won't be disappointed either. Take comfort from the fact that anything you would otherwise be doing would probably be less useful still!

So even if you doubt that your motivation is particularly pure, you are still able to do some good. Avoid self-doubt and inadequacy – that you are too weak or have too much suffering of your own to benefit others, or that giving help to another is draining you of whatever strength you do have. As long as you remain warm and open, that warmth and openness will be returned to some extent. And even if you feel you have failed in helping your partner to relax, you will still have tried and hopefully learned something. It is also possible that this particular person relaxing ever so little is the equivalent of someone with fewer problems relaxing a lot.

PAINTING ♥

If you are able to spend a whole day on Session Seven then, before taking a break for lunch, allow half an hour or so for a free drawing and painting session. Since you have recently been working both inside and outside the skin, it is worth reflecting on some of your discoveries in terms of shapes, patterns and, most importantly, colours. For while there is a lot to be said for discussing and communicating what you have learned to others, there is an equally strong case for finding a more direct way of expressing your feelings on the practice. Words can be tricky. You can say something and believe the words whether what they signify is true or not. It is also possible that you will discover feelings and emotions that you are incapable of putting into words. This is where the language of colour can be especially useful.

The choices we make about colours in respect of our rooms, our clothing, even our car, can be important. They each offer a type of therapeutic nourishment. In the same way, the light visualisations described in this book provide nourishment. So spend 30–40 minutes working with paper, paints, felt-tips or crayons, and enjoy a veritable feast of colour.

There's no need to think of a subject first, just use the colours you like and apply them as you like. Don't worry whether it's art or not because art isn't what you are aiming for. Rather, you are finding a way of drawing out what's going on inside, by brushing, splashing or letting colours drip onto the paper. Neither is there a need to examine the results for any significance. It's your choice of colours and if there is any subject-matter, it's your subject-matter, your hand, your energy behind it. In fact, only you can do whatever it is you do. Only you could leave exactly that kind of mark.

In that sense, this kind of free drawing and painting cannot lie, and if you get into the habit of applying colour to blank paper in this way you will find it does reflect something of yourself in a spontaneous and genuine way, just like a reflection in a mirror. That doesn't mean though that you need to analyse your picture any more than you need to analyse yourself when you catch sight of yourself in a piece of glass.

Of course, not everyone finds it easy to work with colour in this manner, just as some may find it difficult to achieve clarity during the visualisation exercises. That doesn't mean it isn't worth making the effort and taking the time to practise. As with many of the techniques described in this book, repetition allows you to work better and reach deeper. Although you might not want anyone else to see the results of your painting session, what you put down could communicate something to others. First and foremost, though, this time is about spending half an hour or so playing around with colours, simply pleasing yourself, as a child might. Anyone particularly interested in this approach may enjoy a book soon to be published by Carol Sagar, who is one of the Tara Rokpa therapists. Carol is an art therapist who has worked with Akong Rinpoche for many years. This work also relates to such courses as 'Back to Beginnings' and 'Taming the Tiger', which develop a number of the themes suggested in this book, and are recommended to all those wishing to take the work further.

THE LUNCH BREAK

After the painting session you will have earned a long, relaxing lunch break. If you are going to do massage in the afternoon you will need to leave a good hour after eating, so go for a walk perhaps and find a quiet place to sit. Try to bring something of the awareness you found during the session to this free time. Don't rush around doing lots of things or talk too much about what you've discovered. If you're doing this last session within a group there's a case for having some kind of feedback session, or at least a tea-time chat before parting at the end of the day. For now, however, you'll do best simply to take a break. Experience assimilates new information quite naturally, it doesn't need a lot of interpretation. So, if you can, give your discursive mind a break too.

THE AFTERNOON SESSION

Having relaxed for a good hour after eating, all participants in the final session should go through the warm-up exercises outlined on pages 36–42 that work best for them as thoroughly and mindfully as possible. And just as you tried to maintain the relaxed feeling in the post-session period, so you can ease back into it after lunch – or better still try to keep it going throughout the day. You might also like to repeat the pushing hands exercise from page 137, but it's really up to you.

Now you can experience the full body massage as before, only from the other point of view. This should take as long as the first part of the exchange. If you get tired or bored with the simplicity of the situation, try to feel what's happening a little more deeply. If this, too, proves difficult simply follow the in and out-flow of your breath. Even if you just lie there and fall asleep it won't do any harm, but clearly the more you're aware of what's going on, the more you are likely to learn.

OPENNESS VISUALISATION ♥

Following a good long massage and a little rest, you could round off the day with a session of Openness, another visualisation. As you will have practised the breathing and feeling exercises, you may find it relatively simple to ease into a relaxed, aware state, but since this is also a workshop, you might like to check that you are not missing anything out.

So far a very liberal attitude to the practice of massage has been adopted, working exclusively within the bounds of ease and comfort. At no time during the course have your bodies been phys-ically strained or tested. Similarly, rather than pushing yourself to be more than you already are, you will have discovered and devel-oped the positive energy already within – your true nature – and worked with that. However, if you decide to continue learning to relax and sharing that relaxation with others in the future, you might, at some stage, feel like developing your effectiveness still further. As well as directly reducing the amount of suffering in the world, this will also deepen your understanding of the nature of suffering and enhance your ability to relieve it. That isn't to say you have to learn lots of new techniques and massage lots of people. The exercises in this book are very simple, but they can be extraordinarily powerful, according to your motivation and ability to take the practice seriously. So this final section is also something of a celebration because without any great effort you have been able to transform a little of your energy into warm-heartedness towards others. Quite simply and naturally, you are able to generate a little compassion in the world.

Getting comfortable

For this visualisation, lie flat on your back, relaxed and balanced on either side of the spine, or you may want to experiment with sitting upright, cross-legged against a wall, or on a cushion or a chair. Since you are going to be working with the mind, you should try to be comfortable and alert, your breathing free and unconstricted.

Simply sitting and breathing might seem rather a dull business but there's actually quite a lot going on, certainly enough to occupy the attention. Check, for example, that your back is straight, chin tilted to extend the neck, and that your body is balanced symmetrically on either side of the spine. Be aware of the sensation of contact with the floor, the cushion, or the chair, as well as contact with clothing and with the air outside in the room. Note the air flowing into your nostrils, and follow it inside. Take a deep, slow breath, quite full but not forcing anything; count to five as you breathe in, then hold for five, and breathe out for five just as you breathed in. Imagine any stress or tension leaving your body on the out-breath, like emptying a glass of dirty water. Repeat this several times.

Now return to the natural pattern of the breath, only this time focus on the lower abdomen, below the navel. Note how it swells and subsides, observe any sensations associated with this action. Without labelling or naming anything simply notice more and more. And, having noticed, allow yourself to feel what's going on too. Let your mind wander freely through the body, alert to notable sensations. There's bound to be something – a tingling here, perhaps, a dull ache there. If your mind isn't interested, remind it of the importance of the work, renew the motivation; if it wanders, bring it gently back.

Ask yourself what sort of mood you're in – what's the predominant emotional feeling – and whether there's any particular physical sensation that goes along with that. Then take a detached look at your thoughts. Are they fast, jumpy, or slow and even? The aim here isn't to censor or silence the internal dialogue, but just to notice.

Entering the visualisation

Here you are, then, relaxed and aware of one little corner of the Universe. And because you usually have the option of doing something other than just being here, there is now a certain expectancy about the situation. It has potential. As in the previous visualisation exercises, imagine in front of you a completely open sky – either a clear blue day-time sky or a night sky filled with millions of stars. In the centre of this luminous space, imagine a doorway or gateway opening outwards away from you. As you breathe out think that everything inside you – all the thoughts, feelings and experience of the moment – leave you and pass through the gateway into space, where they are transformed into a beautiful golden light, the golden light of universal compassion.

On and outwards the light shines through the gateway in all directions, bringing to everyone everywhere whatever it is they most need and most want. Thus, when the light reaches those who are in pain they are relieved of that pain, while for those who are hungry, the golden light brings food. Whatever is lacking or needed arrives spontaneously with the light. You are not denying or suppressing your own pain and negative emotions here, rather you are acknowledging them as the vital raw materials for the development of true compassion. If you are aware of any particular suffering of your own, as you breathe it through the gate and it transforms into the golden light, you can especially think of others who are suffering in a similar way and send the light first to them. Thus through empathy your own suffering can become useful.

Awakening compassion

The sufferings of old age, sickness, loneliness and disappointment in life are experienced by all of us at various times, but instead of cursing fate or feeling sorry for ourselves, it is possible to relate to this material in a positive and grown-up way. Rather than squirming around helplessly and fearfully in the face of impermanence and mortality, choose to help take care of others instead. In the first instance, the distinction may only be a state of mind, but with practice that positive intention can inform and illumine your entire perception of reality.

This may seem like a big step from living more or less single-mindedly. We are so used to trying to acquire and maintain whatever it is that we think will make us happy that it can be difficult to feel quite so motivated about working for the benefit of others. In this case, you could visualise those you love beyond the gateway and empathise with their suffering, shine the golden light on them. That warm glow you feel when you think of a person you love is natural warmth and goodness, the working basis.

Another approach is to think about your own suffering and consider all others who have similar problems, only worse. You hate the noise your neighbour makes, for example, but then again you might be deaf. It may be a cliché that there's always someone worse off, but it's true. And since you are discovering that you have much more confidence and richness than you thought, it's safe to assume that the vast majority of beings are, in a sense, worse off than you. Allow the light to go out to all who come to mind.

The natural warmth, the basic goodness within, was always, is always and will always be there, it's just a question of awakening it. Whether you are moved by love, logic, empathy, despair or disappointment is not so important, so long as you are moved to feel compassion and are prepared to practise expressing and developing it. The object of your compassion can be the real person beyond the gateway, in the golden light, not merely an image or a hologram. You can shine your light on others as literally as you like, even when or after they are no longer with you. In fact, compassion, as well as being warm, beneficial and indestructible, is also limitless in terms of time and space. A kind thought for someone who died twenty years ago, or who is currently on the other side of the world, is as valid as concern for someone currently sharing the same room with you.

The openness visualisation is also designed to extend that awakening into your everyday consciousness. For this kind of exercise is self-supporting. Just as your ideas, feeling, impulses and intentions lead to action in the physical world of your everyday life, so visualisation techniques can create the model for a more compassionate and mature attitude at all levels of our being, and in all situations.

Furthering the visualisation

As you breathe out, imagine that all your suffering and disappointment, however trivial, is transformed into golden light as it passes through the gate. And as this antidote to suffering touches others who are suffering and grants them whatever they need to release them from it, try to feel rather than simply to think that this is happening; try fully to experience rather than watch the process. And since what is being transformed is pain and disappointment rather than your store of goodness being used up, you can afford to shine as much light for as long as you can.

At the end, the golden light fills the whole Universe and touches every single being with its compassion and this includes you. Allow yourself to feel the golden light finally coming to you, bringing whatever you most want and need. Then just rest for a little while, allowing your thoughts to come and go freely without any restriction. For a long moment or two, feel the absence of any conflict, or even distinction between the spaces outside and inside of you. That is openness.

You are not looking for the practice to have any particular effect here, remember. For example, someone you have bathed in your light isn't suddenly going to recover from illness or phone you up out of the blue. But they might. And your attitude to the one in question will certainly improve.

For some people it's natural to think of all those who need help and imagine them quite literally receiving whatever they need. Others may find it easier to visualise that every time they breathe out, their experience and potential is transformed into something pure and beneficial in a rather more abstract sense. In either case, I feel bound to say that in my experience this kind of positive thinking can have a powerful effect on the lives of those who practise it, and on the lives of all those associated with them. It is my sincere hope that you will discover this yourself. And if you can bring some of that openness into your everyday dealings with other people and situations, then learning to relax will have been worthwhile.

REFLECTIONS AT THE END OF THE DAY

Now that you have completed your day of massage and relaxation, you may wish to reflect a little as a group, or on your own or with your friend, on the value of this work as you have experienced it. A cup of tea may help you with this. You may just want to appreciate the occasion or you may want to discuss the possibility of going further with this work. You may decide that you want to make contact with one of the Tara Rokpa therapists or perhaps you have worked as much as you feel is useful with this approach in a formal sense. Informally though, no doubt whatever you have put into this work, it will continue to grow within you and in your relationships with other people. Even the smallest increase in awareness and compassion in any individual is a significant contribution to us all.

A few final thoughts on how you might wish to develop this work for yourself. Some people may feel at this stage that they really should study anatomy before working with other people's bodies. While a working knowledge of anatomy and physiology is very useful, it can only provide a map or model for the human body and its functioning. In fact, some members of the medical profession who have spent years studying these subjects, have no idea how to touch people effectively. As a result, they can help less in certain situations than an uneducated person who has simply developed the art of touching well.

Furthermore, being aware that you don't know much beyond what you feel in the moment can be the ground of true humility. It will help you to remember always to work with care and respect for the other person, in case you could accidentally do them some harm. However, there will come a moment when you will probably wish to seek out a class or a few texts on anatomy and physiology. At that point, your interest and understanding of the subject will be greatly enhanced by the work you have already done with simple massage and self-massage.

My advice is not to be in any great hurry to acquire more and more knowledge of the subject, but rather to try and stabilise your experience of these very basic and simple techniques. Then as questions arise about the body, seek out books and individuals whose approach seem wholesome and thorough. Be wary of any book or person making miraculous claims for their special way of understanding the body.

Whatever you are engaged in, you have more to offer when you feel open and relaxed and have let go of some of your tension and worry. You can spare a moment any time and any place for a little sitting, experiencing breath and feelings, either when stress is felt or before it gets to that stage. In fact, you should try to make it a habit. If you have an inexplicable resistance to just sitting, remember that nothing really is the hardest thing to do. So be very patient in your attempts and keep them very short.

Learn to trust yourself and be prepared to offer it. You may know you are often very stressed, but you don't have to wait until you can relax completely before you find you have something to share. I don't think it's an exaggeration to say that many of us would have to wait until we were dead. As long as you can continue to develop this precious link between inner peace and openness and the wish and willingness to share what little you have, then the process of learning and maturing happens naturally.

Afterword:
looking to the millennium

Writing as I am on the brink of the last year of the twentieth century, it is almost impossible not to think what may be the implications of this work for the new millennium. My own feeling is that healing relaxation (of course, I don't just mean this book) will be of ever-increasing importance in the years to come.

There seems to be no limit to the amount of pressure that modern life has to offer. If you think back to your own childhood you will remember that life was very different. If I were to sum it up for myself I'd say that there is more speed and less space. Both of these factors have a very big effect on how I feel in the world and on the outer environment.

Though I was a crusader for good causes when I was younger, I now accept that many things will not revert to the way I would prefer them to be. The high-rise buildings that crowd the thoroughfares of the community where I grew up will not be turned back into houses with lawns and stands of trees and shrubs. Streets now crowded with three lanes of traffic will not change back into a place where it's safe for a child to learn to ride a bike. Houses and neighbourhoods where the people make the music instead of through radios, TVs and CD players are not likely to be found, even in far-off India or Tibet. Conversation centred on people's own experience rather than on what has been garnered from 'the media' in up-to-the-minute reports is harder and harder to find. The need to rush doesn't seem to be my problem alone. So what do we need to do about too much speed and not enough space?

The answer seems to lie in being prepared to work with life just as it comes, not hating it because it seems so awful in comparison with some memory or fantasy. It requires learning to be present. In the present moment, there is always space and no such thing as speed. How it is is just that: *as it is*. As soon as I am prepared to deal with myself and everything else in life on that basis, then and only then can I relax.

In the new millennium, to accept things just as they are – to relax – will mean to be willing to face extremes. Though it is nice when we are able to create little oases of peace and harmony to share with others, we should not make too much effort to achieve this harmony. Even if we achieve it, trying to maintain it will make us very tense indeed.

Looking over this book I realise that in passing on so much good advice, I may at points give the impression that I am a naturally relaxed and compassionate person. This is not the case. In fact, it is more the situation of a teacher knowing how to teach maths because of having had such a hard time learning it. But in spite of having learned so little of all I've been taught, when it comes to the development of relaxation and compassion, even one drop extra is valuable in this world. I have no regrets in having made this development the main project of my life. I hope it will be the same for all of you.

London
1 October 1998

About Rokpa

Rokpa is the Tibetan word for 'help' and is the name of a world-wide group of organisations dedicated to improving the quality of life in the developed and developing world. Rokpa has no political or sectarian aims and is wholly dedicated to the relief of suffering and enrichment of life.

Rokpa's activities worldwide include: soup kitchens in Europe, Africa and Nepal; primary, secondary, medical education and teacher training in Tibet; and tree planting in the Himalayas and on Holy Island in Scotland.

All these projects were set up under the inspiration of Dr Akong Tulku Rinpoche, Rokpa's founder. They are united by one motivation: helping where help is needed.

Rokpa International is based in Zurich, Switzerland, and distributes funds to the developing world. It has associated fundraising branches in more than 15 countries in Europe, North America, Africa and Asia. All branches are staffed by volunteers. The Zurich office is headed up by Rokpa's vice-president, Ms Lea Wyler, who is also director of projects in Nepal and who helped start Rokpa in 1980.

The link of Tara Rokpa Therapy to other Rokpa projects is also found by many to be therapeutic. Much illness and mental distress is related to a cut-off condition. Joining together to help others and participating in spiritually based activities can often be part of a healing process.

For more information about Rokpa contact Rokpa Trust, Kagyu Samye Ling, Eskdalemuir, Nr Langholm, Dumfriesshire, DG13 0QL, Scotland. Telephone: 013873 73232 or e-mail: charity@rokpa.u-net.com; website: http://www.rokpa.u-net.com.

About Tara Rokpa Therapy and therapy training

Tara Rokpa Therapy has developed from the insights of Dr Akong Tulku Rinpoche working in conjunction with the five Western therapists listed in the Useful Addresses as senior Tara Rokpa therapists. The sequence of exercises and activities given in this book constitute the first and most basic component of Tara Rokpa Therapy. It is presented to groups in a course form called Beginning to Relax. As this book makes clear, relaxation is to a healthy, happy life what flour is to bread. So Beginning to Relax, as presented by Tara Rokpa therapists, is a valuable process that can stand on its own.

Some people feel they wish to continue with this approach as a journey towards self-understanding and compassion for all. At a time when psychotherapy is coming under scrutiny in all countries, Tara Rokpa Therapy attempts to pass on to individuals a way of coming to know that they can be their own best therapist.

Tara Rokpa Therapy groups are active at present in about ten countries worldwide. Under the guidance of Tara Rokpa – trained therapists, group members progress through stages of the method: Beginning to Relax, Back to Beginnings, Taming the Tiger, Six Lights and Six Realms, and Compassion Year. The groups move at different speeds depending on the needs of the members. Tara Rokpa Therapy can also be undertaken by individuals under the guidance of a Tara Rokpa therapist.

Tara Rokpa Therapy has also generated a four-year psychotheraphy training for those who wish to train in greater depth in these methods. Most who have undertaken the training thus far are already health care professionals, while others seek to have this as their principal qualification. If you would like to know more about the Tara Rokpa Therapy contact Tara Rokpa, Edinburgh at the address on the page 179, or one of the therapists in your area.

Useful addresses

Tara Rokpa Edinburgh
250 Ferry Road
Edinburgh EH5 3AN
Scotland
UK

Tel/fax: 44- (0) 131 552 1431
e-mail: tara-rok@tara-rok.demon.co.uk

Dr Akong Tulku Rinpoche
Kagyu Samye Ling
Eskdalemuir nr Langholm
Dumfriesshire DG13 0QL
Scotland
UK

Tel: 44- (0) 13873 73232
Fax: 44- (0) 13873 73223

Senior Tara Rokpa therapists

Dorothy Gunne MA, M.psych.Sc. (Psychotherapy), A.F.P.s.S.I.
8 Granite Terrace
Inchicore
Dublin 8
Eire

Tel: 353- (1) 454 2453
e-mail: dorothy.gunne@ntdi.ie

Edie Irwin, MA, IAHIP
c/o Tara Rokpa Edinburgh

or

c/o Dublin Samye Dzong
56 Inchicore Road
Dublin 8
Eire

or

c/o Rokpa, USA
6501 Gretna Green Way
Alexandria VA 22312
USA

Tel: 1- (703) 642 2248
Fax: 1- (703) 642 1591
e-mail: rokpa.usa@ibm.net

Carol Sagar B.A. Hons. A.T.C., Dip.A.Th, R.A.Th.
The Maisonette
St Cecilia's
13 Sea View Road
Mundesley
Norfolk NR11 8DH

Tel/fax: 44- (0) 1263 721 493

Dr Brion Sweeney, M.B.M. Med.Sc. (Psychotherapy),
M.R.C.Psych.
4 Grattan Court
Inchicore
Dublin 8
Eire

Tel: 353- (1) 454 5923
Fax: 353- (1) 453 5021
email: b.sweeney@indigo.ie

Trish Swift, M.Soc.Sc, M.S.S., S.Sc.
Rokpa Zimbabwe
34/31 Quendon Road
Monavale
PO Mabelreign
Harare
Zimbabwe

Tel: 263- (4) 304 411
e-mail: sharad@zol.co.zw

Junior Tara Rokpa therapists

Annie Dibble, B.A., IAHIP
24 North Terrace
Inchicore
Dublin 8
Eire

Tel/fax: 353- (1) 453 7304

Lorna Hensey, B.Soc.Sc., S.R.N.
Millhill Cottage
Corsock
Castle Douglas
Kirkcudbrightshire
DG7 3DP
Scotland

Tel: 44- (0) 1644 440 280

Dr Ulrich Kuestner, MD
Schluterstrasse 9
10625 Berlin
Germany

Tel/fax: 49- (30) 31503883
e-mail: uku@snafu.de

Senior trainees

Stephan Storm, M.A. Psych.
Heistrebarg 3a
25725 Schafstedt
Germany

Tel: 49- (0) 4805 695
e-mail: stephan@iol.ie

Lorna Watson
Rosehall
Lochmaben
Nr Lockerbie
Dumfriesshire
DG11 1RJ

Tel/fax: 44- (0) 1387 811 561

Tara Rokpa Therapy country representatives

Claudia Wellnitz
Bahnhofstrasse 13
Valtern 1- 9052
Italy

Tel: 34- (471) 964 183
e-mail: c.well@iol.it

Maria Creixell
c/o Samye Dzong Barcelona
Pau Claris No. 74, 2
08010 Barcelona
Spain

Tel/fax: 34- (93) 301 5472

Marjorie Epp, B.A. (Psych.)
133 Sicamore Place
Fort McMurray
Alberta T9H 3RY
Canada

Tel: 1- (403) 743 5774
e-mail: kelmar@telusplanet.net

Marie-France Kunlin
11 rue Baillou
75014 Paris
France

Tel: 33- (0) 1 45 423 833

Gregorz Bral and Anna Zubrzycka
Rokpa Polska
20-437 Lublin
W.Nadrzecczna 57/3
Poland

Tel/fax: 48- (81) 744 5235

Further reading

The titles listed below are hardly the only possible choice. The books are a compilation of old friends and new discoveries which may help you in your explorations.

Acupressure

Acupressure by Carola Beresford-Cooke, Macmillan, *Naturally Better* Series, Quarto.

Aikido

The Art of Peace: Teachings of the Founder of Aikido by Morihei Ueshiba, John Stevens (translator), Shambhala Pocket Classics, 1992.

Ki in Aikido: A Sampler of Ki Exercises by Linda Adkisson and CM Shifflett, 1998.

Anatomy

Anatomy and Physiology (Healthcare Professional Guides) by Springhouse Corp., Springhouse Publishing Co, 1998.

Aromatherapy

The Art of Aromatherapy by Robert B Tisserand, CW Daniel, 1977.

The Complete Illustrated Guide to Aromatherapy: A Practical Approach to the use of Essential Oils for Health and Well-being by Julia Lawless, Element, 1997.

Do-*in* and self-massage

Book of Do-In by Michio Kuchi, Japan Publications, Inc., 1979.

Do-in 2: A Most Complete Work on the Ancient Art of Self-massage by Jacques de Langre, Happiness Press.

The Self-Shiatsu Book by Pamela Ferguson, Newleaf, 1996.

Massage

The Book of Massage: The Complete Step-by-step Guide to Eastern and Western Techniques by Lucinda Lidell et al, Simon & Schuster, 1984.

Compassionate Touch: Hands-on Caregiving for the Elderly, the Ill and the Dying by Dawn Nelson, Talman Company, 1993.

The Massage Book by George Downing, Random House, 1972.

Massage for Beginners by Marilyn Aslani, HarperCollins, 1997.

The Modern Book of Massage by Anne Kent Rush and Byron Preiss, Stonework Ltd (Dell), 1994.

Tappan's Handbook of Healing Massage Techniques by Frances Tappan and Patricia Benjamin; Prentice Hall International, 1998.

Meditation

Cutting through Spiritual Materialism by Chogyam Trungpa Rinpoche, Shambhala Press, 1987.

Openness Mind by Tarthang Tulku, Dharma Publishing.

Start from Where You Are by Ani Pema Chodron, Shambhala Press.

Taming the Tiger by Akong Tulku Rinpoche, Rider Press, 1998.

Reflexology

Original Works of Eunice D Ingham: *Stories the Feet Can Tell Through Reflexology/Stories the Feet have told through Reflexology* by Eunice D Ingham, Dwight C Byers, Ingham, 1984.

Reflexology: Art, Science and History by Christine Issel, New Frontier, 1996.

Reflexology: A Step-by-step Guide by Nicola M Hall, Caro Ness (Editor), Element, 1997.

The Reflexology Manual: An Easy-to-Use Illustrated Guide to the Healing Zones of the Hands and Feet by Pauline Wills, Healing Arts Press, 1995.

Tai Chi

Embrace Tiger Return to Mountain by Al Huang, Celestial Arts, 1995.

Yoga

Light on Yoga by BKS Iyengar, Schocken Books (Random House).

Yoga Over 50 by Mary Stewart, Little Brown, 1995.

Tara Rokpa publications and recordings

Back to Beginnings by Edie Irwin (Tara Rokpa Edinburgh, 1993)

Working with the Elements by Edie Irwin (Tara Rokpa Edinburgh, 1993)

Beginning to Relax (an audio cassette of relaxation exercises) by Edie Irwin (Tara Rokpa Edinburgh)

Tara Rokpa Summer Camp, Germany, 1998 (videos of evening lectures) by Akong Tulku Rinpoche and Tara Rokpa Therapists (Kagyu Samye Ling, 1998)

Acknowledgements

I want to thank many, many people for their generosity and support in all imaginable dimensions of my life over so many years. Knowing that I am excluding most, I will name a few without whom this book could never have come to be.

Dr Akong Tulku Rinpoche: my supreme guide and mentor in this life, whose living compassion, humility and humour are matchless.

My family: especially my late father Donald Irwin, who as a newspaper reporter set out to discover and write the truth on a deadline day after day for fifty years and my mother Polly Irwin, who continues to be unceasingly encouraging to all her children in our diverse ventures.

In memoriam: Dr R. D. Laing who first introduced me to the profound importance of relaxation as the basis for knowing the nature of the human mind. His high standards in all aspects of human endeavour I have taken as a touchstone for my own. I remain most especially grateful to him for insisting on the primacy of direct experience in determining the value of life.

Colin Betts: whose extraordinary contribution is told in the foreword to this book.

Marita Weimar: who, with Sylvia Wetzel's help, caught the images for this work first on film and then in her sensitive drawings. Also Pat Murphy, David Casby and friends in Dublin for helping to clarify the illustrative requirements for the book.

Sean McGovern: my companion and support during the run-up to the retreat who with his kind and discriminating judgement and genuine friendship remains a valuable resource in my life.

My colleagues in the work of Tara Rokpa Therapy: Dot Gunne, Carol Sagar, Brion Sweeney, and Trish Swift; Annie Dibble, Lorna Hensey, Uli Kuestner, Stephan Storm, Harriet Trevelyan, and Lorna Watson, all of whom have taken much time and trouble to supply me with valuable feedback and criticism based on their use of this text in work with groups. To all trainees and clients, indeed all those who have shared in the development of this work.

Also available from Rider ...

TAMING THE TIGER
Tibetan Teachings for Improving Daily Life
Akong Tulku Rinpoche

Taming the Tiger offers a simple approach to finding happiness for oneself that also brings happiness to others.

In the first half of the book, Akong Rinpoche explains common-sense principles of the Buddhist view as they may be applied in everyday life. The advice given speaks to anyone seeking the truth about happiness and suffering.

The second half consists of a sequence of meditational exercises which, if practised consistently, will provide a basis for self-knowledge, mind therapy and self healing which will continue throughout one's life.

This practical programme has been tested and refined first at the therapy workshops of Samye Ling in Scotland and has since confirmed its success all over the world.

If you would like to order any of the following or to receive our catalogue please fill in the form below:

Taming the Tiger by Akong Tulku Rinpoche	£9.99
Enlightened Management by Dona Witten with Akong Tulku Rinpoche	£9.99
The Tibetan Book of Living and Dying by Sogyal Rinpoche	£7.99
Inner Revolution by Robert Thurman	£12.99
A Path With Heart by Jack Kornfield	£6.99
Buddha's Little Instruction Book by Jack Kornfield	£6.99
The Complete Relaxation Book by James Hewitt	£9.99
The Complete Yoga Book by James Hewitt	£9.99
The Little Book of Inner Space by Stafford Whiteaker	£1.99
The Little Book of Happiness by Patrick Whiteside	£1.99

HOW TO ORDER

BY POST: TBS Direct, TBS Ltd, Colchester Road, Frating Green, Essex CO7 7DW

Please send me _____ copies of _____ @ £ _____ each

☐ I enclose my cheque for £ _____ payable to Rider Books

☐ Please charge £ _____ to my American Express/Visa/Mastercard account*
    (*delete as applicable)

Card No ☐☐☐☐☐☐☐☐☐☐☐☐☐☐☐☐☐☐☐

Expiry Date: ☐☐☐☐☐   Signature _____

Name _____

Address _____

_____ Postcode _____

Delivery address if different _____

_____ Postcode _____

Or call our credit card hotline on 01206 255800.

Please have your card details handy.

Please quote reference: LightE1

 Rider is an imprint of Random House UK Ltd

Please tick here if you do not wish to receive further information from Rider or associated companies ☐